D0131629

Be Your Own Boss

By Marcia Passos Duffy

WetFeet Insider Guide

Helping you make smarter career decisions.

WetFeet, Inc.

The Folger Building
101 Howard Street
Suite 300
San Francisco, CA 94105

Phone: (415) 284-7900 or 1-800-926-4JOB
Fax: (415) 284-7910
Website: www.wetfeet.com

Be Your Own Boss

By Marcia Passos Duffy
ISBN: 1-58207-537-9

Table of Contents

Introduction

What is it like to freelance for a living? Imagine this: You ditch your high heels and business suits for whatever work attire suits your fancy: sweatpants, jeans, a T-shirt—yes, even bunny slippers. You "commute" to your office in less than 30 seconds. You throw in a load of laundry between calls, repot plants during your lunch break, stay in bed when you're sick—without the guilt—and bring your laptop and cell phone to the park with your kids.

But talk to any working freelancer and you'll realize that while *in theory* you can do any of these things while working from home, reality often gets in the way of a cushy lifestyle.

An important client calls while your child is howling with strep throat. Another customer hasn't settled his account in three months and you need the money—now—to pay the mortgage. You're so frantic with a deadline you haven't left the house in three days except to stick your head out the door to sign a UPS slip. You've worked six months straight without a break, but are now in a month-long lull that's keeping you up at night.

Bottom line: Freelancing is a mixed bag. And whether you survive or go back to corporate life depends on how well you tolerate the downside to working on your own—as well as how you handle the perks.

WHAT IS A FREELANCER?

The word freelance comes from the medieval term for a mercenary soldier, a "free lance"; in other words, a soldier who was not attached to any particular master or government and could be hired for the task at hand (the lance was his weapon). The military analogy doesn't necessarily fit the modern-day freelancer, but the part about not being beholden to any master certainly resonates.

Freelancers, consultants, and independent contractors are terms that are often casually thrown around but mean basically the same thing: marketing your skills, knowledge, and talent to potential clients who hire you to work on a specific project or projects.

Contract work and freelancing are essentially one and the same—though a contract project can imply that the work is longer-term than a freelance project might be. A consultant is a freelancer who sells his or her expertise and advises a course of action. Many freelancers with skills such as writing, pet training, graphic design, or computer programming also do consulting work to supplement their income. All in all, being a freelancer means you sell *services*, not products.

Whatever you decide to call yourself, only "independent contractor" has meaning in the eyes of the U.S. Internal Revenue Service; it's what you need to use when filing your tax return. In a nutshell, this simply means that you perform a service for a client in exchange for a fee, but you're not an employee of the client. The client has control of the *result* of the work performed by an independent contractor; the independence comes in with the *means and methods* of accomplishing a project. In other words, a client can tell you *what* to do (and when it's due—read: deadlines), but not *how* you do it (or *when* you work).

Don't confuse freelancing with being an entrepreneur. While it takes a healthy dose of entrepreneurial spirit to be a freelancer, true entrepreneurs are on a completely different wavelength. The goal of the entrepreneur is to create a corporation larger than himself—with investors, employees, and big growth. If you are a true freelancer, the mere thought of expanding your business might be enough to make you cringe. Freelancers typically want to be "free" of corporate life—and all that goes along with it. Most would never dream of expanding beyond their own offices.

WHO'S FREELANCING AND WHY?

Freelancing used to be the domain of highly creative people in bustling metropolitan areas. But technological advances and the Internet have changed all of that and opened the doors for new freelancing opportunities. Today you'll find freelance computer programmers, personal trainers, and financial planners among all of those writers, graphic designers, and photographers. New types of jobs that are perfect for home-based work are springing up as well, such as virtual assistants (online executive assistants/secretaries), daily money managers (those who help people too busy to manage their household finances or not interested in doing so), and life coaches (trained professionals who provide guidance on life issues either face-to-face or via email or phone).

People turn to freelancing for a wide variety of reasons—from corporate downsizing to becoming a parent, to wanting to try out something new, to the death of a spouse. Freedom from the constraints of a traditional 9-to-5 job, however, is a recurring theme.

Pinning down the exact number of people working in the United States as freelancers is not an easy feat, even for the statistics experts: Numbers range from 8.6 million (recorded by the Bureau of Labor Statistics) to as high as 20 million (the number of businesses filing Schedule Cs with their federal income taxes. Schedule C is a form intended for sole proprietors and independent contractors to report profits and losses from business activities).

Experts do agree, however, that more people are entering the freelance pool every day.

"There's no question that freelancing is an increasing trend," says Gene Fairbrother, lead small-business consultant for the National Association of the Self-Employed, and ShopTalk 800 columnist for the organization's magazine, *Self-Employed America*. Fairbrother notes that while many people set up shop as freelancers, not everyone makes it. "There's a wash going in and out of freelancing… but overall, there are more people making it since there is growth."

Jane M. Lommel, PhD, president of Workforce Associates, a consulting firm that works with organizations in the public and private sectors in the areas of workforce and economic development, agrees that the freelancing ranks have increased in the past five years, probably due to the recession and its concomitant corporate downsizing. "Anecdotally, we know that more people are turning to their own expertise and hanging out their shingles," she says. This trend will only increase as the baby boomers age and choose phased retirement over full retirement, she notes.

According to Bureau of Labor Statistics (BLS) data, the typical freelancer is an experienced professional (usually 35-plus) who holds at least a bachelor's degree.

On average, solo business owners earn more per week than traditional salaried workers ($523 per week compared to $510 respectively). And intangible rewards are even greater: The vast majority of freelancers surveyed by the BLS say they are happy with their work. Eighty-three percent say they prefer their freelance life to traditional employment.

Those who venture into the freelance world generally fall into three categories:

1. **Full-timers:** Those who work as freelancers exclusively. Some start as *toe-dippers* (see following), but eventually become successful enough to quit their full-time jobs.

2. **Toe-dippers:** People who try freelancing part-time while still maintaining their full-time jobs.

3. **Fence-sitters:** Those who truly want to freelance, but for whatever reasons—be they financial or otherwise—never quite make the move. They may tinker with the idea, sometimes even taking on freelance projects, but never actually leave their full-time job in corporate America.

Are you a fence-sitter? If so, this book is intended to get you off the fence... and maybe even propel you toward a rewarding full-time freelance life.

MY OWN FREELANCE JOURNEY

Unlike most things I've fantasized about in my life, my freelance flight of fancy—now a reality for ten years—is one of the best decisions I ever made.

I had been working in New York City as a writer and account executive for medium-sized public relations firms. By the time I left, I was an account supervisor making decent money with a pretty nice office overlooking the Empire State Building. I was also smoking two packs of cigarettes and drinking a gallon of coffee per day and, at one point, commuting nearly two hours to work.

I began freelancing quite by accident when my family and I moved out of the New York metropolitan area into a small city in New England—a deliberate flight from the pressures of urban life. Once we settled in, I was hired by the local newspaper as a part-time correspondent covering events for several outlying towns.

When I arrived at the newsroom for my first day at work, I learned that part-time stringers don't get a desk—or even a computer or phone. I would have to work out of a conference room and wait for a computer to free up after deadline. After contemplating this for a minute, I tiptoed up to my editor, who was under the gun to put out the day's edition of the newspaper, and asked if I could go home and work. "Sure, go ahead," he said, without even looking up. I headed back home, set up an office, and haven't left since. While I worked for many years as a correspondent, I soon realized that I could make more money doing other writing gigs as well. My freelance career was born.

And how does my day look now? I have no one looking over my shoulder (unless you count my non-judgmental house pets). My commute is approximately half a minute from my upstairs bedroom to my downstairs office. I take many detours—helping my kids get ready for the day, picking up clothing, getting breakfast ready, and walking my son to school. Then I take the dog for a 45-minute romp through the neighboring woods. I settle at my desk at 10 a.m. My coworkers, the cats, arrive before me, and often vie for a position on my lap or across my desk. And my office manager, the dog, promptly falls asleep on her ottoman. I check my email, and work on various writing projects until noon, when I have lunch. I continue working until 3:00 when I pick up my son, and my daughter comes home from school. If the kids have play dates or other activities, I can squeeze in another hour of work before dinner. I sometimes work an hour or two after the kids have gone to bed, for a total of six to nine hours a day.

My job allows me to be there for my kids. I can enjoy my house. I can watch the changing seasons from my office window overlooking the garden. I feel connected to the community. I don't miss the office politics, the pressure of dressing for success, or even the water-cooler gossip. I have found my perfect career. I can say, without hesitation, that I love my job.

Working for myself has allowed me to explore different ways to keep my career interesting and fun. As a freelance journalist, I've written stories about everything from dairy farming to lawn care to camping with kids to throwing a sushi party. I've also written for companies—brochures, press releases, publicity strategy. My solo career has enabled me to pursue my dream of having my own online magazine, which I publish weekly. I've also branched into writing personal histories with another writer; we interview elders and put together books on their stories for their families. I doubt that this kind of creative job exploration would fly if I were on staff at a company.

Having an office in your home is quite different from getting up, getting dressed, and leaving it all behind to commute to an office somewhere else. It took me almost three years to get the balance just right. Was it worth it? Yes. Would I go back to working for someone else? Not if I can help it. While freelancing is not for everyone, if you can make it work, it can be the most fulfilling way of combining your personal and professional lives.

So what does it take to join the millions of people who freelance for a living? This book will walk you step-by-step through that lovely fantasy of working in your sweats and slippers, and help turn it into a reality. But first, it'll help you thoroughly explore what's involved and decide whether freelancing is right for you.

Our self-assessment tests in the first chapter will help you ask yourself if you're cut out for the freelancing lifestyle, as well as discuss some reasons why you should—or shouldn't—go solo. We'll review careers suited to freelancing and how to turn what you love to do into a full-time gig. This book will also help you figure out what you need to have in place before you hand in your resignation, and what to consider seriously before taking the leap. Our real-people profiles will give you a real feel for the freelance life on the day-to-day level.

Be aware that freelancing isn't for everyone—or for every profession. But it could be for you. So if you think it's time to take the plunge into freelancing, read on and gather the tools you'll need to get started.

Is Freelancing For You?

Top Five Freelancing Myths

Is Freelancing for You? Take the Test

The Necessary Traits

Insider Scoop

What does it take to go solo? The first order of business is to get a good dose of reality. Let's quickly dispel some of the common myths surrounding freelancing. Then you can take the self-assessment test to find out if you truly have a freelancer's spirit and to help you decide if this is the path for you.

Top Five Freelancing Myths

MYTH #1: YOU DON'T HAVE A BOSS

True, you don't have *a* boss; rather, you have *many* bosses—your clients, various organizations, the tax man, and yourself. While you won't have someone literally looking over your shoulder and assigning you tasks, you will have to deliver to your customers or clients who, instead of giving you a bad review if you don't do a good job, may never work with you again—and refuse to pay you.

MYTH #2: IT'S EASY WORK AND YOU MAKE TONS OF MONEY

It's easy in the sense that work doesn't feel "hard" when you love what you do. But you may soon discover that you've never worked harder in your life. Even if you've had tough bosses in the past, you'll probably be your own personal slave driver. Expect to work at least 40 hours a week—if not more—particularly when you begin. "A lot of people have this misconception that freelancers make a killing because they charge more per hour than someone makes in a company," says one public relations consultant. "But people don't consider that you have to pay your own health insurance, be your own bill collector, and more."

MYTH #3: YOU'LL HAVE LOTS OF FREE TIME

It would be more accurate to say that you'll have a very flexible schedule. You will have the freedom to go to the gym when you want to without having to answer to anyone, but you'll quickly realize that every hour spent not working must be made up at some other time—often at night. "I could be running errands all day and people [I run into] think I'm not working," says one freelance writer. "But they don't see that I go home and put in eight to nine hours of work…. I just do it at different hours."

It's certainly not true that you'll be able to spend lots of time with your children while you work. This notion is perpetuated by the staged photos of "work at home" companies that display women sitting with happy, placid toddlers on their laps. "You can't work at home and take care of your children all of the time," says one insider with two kids. "I have always needed a sitter at least some of the time to guarantee that I'll get some work done."

> **A lot of people have this misconception that freelancers make a killing because they charge more per hour than someone makes in a company. But people don't consider that you have to pay your own health insurance, be your own bill collector, and more.**

MYTH #4: YOU WON'T BE INTERRUPTED WORKING AT HOME

You may not have coworkers stopping by to chat or meetings filling up your daily planner, but you can bet that you'll likely get interrupted many times a day not just for work-related issues, but also for issues associated with your personal life, by repair people, sick children, or spouses. And once your neighbors know you're home, they may ask you to do any number of favors, such as letting workers into their homes or taking care of their kids after school. Still, despite the interruptions, many freelancers say that they're able to get a lot more done working at home than in an office. "I can accomplish something in two hours at home that would normally take me four hours to complete in an office," says a freelance public relations consultant.

MYTH #5: YOU WON'T HAVE TO DEAL WITH OFFICE POLITICS

You won't have to deal with the stressful day-to-day backbiting and gossip around the water cooler, but if your clients are in a business or office setting you can bet that, in some way, you'll be affected by office politics and culture. And your lack of knowledge about what's going on in the office can sometimes work against you. One public relations insider says he lost a client because he was unaware that the great publicity he was generating for one executive was causing jealousy in the ranks. Yet, as one business consultant puts it, not being on the inside has its advantages: "I can come into a company from the outside and point things out that people on the inside can't for political reasons.…That's the piece I love.…I don't have to pretend that certain problems don't exist."

Is Freelancing for You?
Take the Test

At least eight primary personality traits are needed to succeed in a freelance career. You don't have to start out strong in every trait; some of these traits are actually skills that can be learned. Plus, different fields require strengths in different areas. (We'll discuss these later.)

Take this self-assessment test to find out where you stand. Answer the following statements honestly:

 FREELANCE ASSESSMENT TEST

1. I feel comfortable working alone.

   a) True

   b) Sometimes true

   c) False

2. I am motivated to start a project by myself. No one has to tell me what to do.

   a) True

   b) Sometimes true

   c) False

FREELANCE ASSESSMENT TEST, CONT'D

3. I'll take over a project if I have to, but I feel more comfortable with someone else in charge.

   a) True

   b) Sometimes true

   c) False

4. I don't mind working ten- to twelve-hour days if it will help me stay on top of my game.

   a) True

   b) Sometimes true

   c) False

5. I'm eager and willing to learn and do things that may fall outside of my area of expertise.

   a) True

   b) Sometimes true

   c) False

6. I'm tired of working so hard at my job. I'd like to have more free time.

   a) True

   b) Sometimes true

   c) False

7. I'm okay when I make mistakes. I can pick myself up and bounce back.

   a) True

   b) Sometimes true

   c) False

FREELANCE ASSESSMENT TEST

8. I feel very discouraged when things don't go as expected.

   a) True

   b) Sometimes true

   c) False

9. I have a hard time making decisions.

   a) True

   b) Sometimes true

   c) False

10. I prefer a steady paycheck so that I know how much money I have coming in, and when.

    a) True

    b) Sometimes true

    c) False

11. I love coming up with creative solutions to problems. I tend to naturally invent new ways of doing things.

    a) True

    b) Sometimes true

    c) False

12. I like to have my workday planned out so that I know exactly what's on my agenda. I get frustrated when last-minute projects are thrown in.

    a) True

    b) Sometimes true

    c) False

FREELANCE ASSESSMENT TEST, CONT'D

13. I have a lot of experience and knowledge in my field.

    a) True

    b) Sometimes true

    c) False

14. I know what it takes to run a business day to day.

    a) True

    b) Sometimes true

    c) False

15. I think freelancers should hire out their administrative tasks, and just focus on the work that they're good at.

    a) True

    b) Sometimes true

    c) False

16. I'm good at staying organized and planning ahead.

    a) True

    b) Sometimes true

    c) False

17. I work well with deadlines and finish projects on time.

    a) True

    b) Sometimes true

    c) False

FREELANCE ASSESSMENT TEST

18. I find it hard to stick to a planned daily schedule. I'm easily distracted by immediate concerns.

    a) True

    b) Sometimes true

    c) False

19. I love networking and sharing ideas. I'm well connected in my community.

    a) True

    b) Sometimes true

    c) False

20. I feel comfortable saying "I don't know" to a question, and then finding out the answer.

    a) True

    b) Sometimes true

    c) False

21. I'm shy and don't really like approaching strangers.

    a) True

    b) Sometimes true

    c) False

22. Success, for me, is not measured by money.

    a) True

    b) Sometimes true

    c) False

FREELANCE ASSESSMENT TEST, CONT'D

23. I prefer a well-paying, stable job, even if it doesn't necessarily fulfill my dreams.

    a) True

    b) Sometimes true

    c) False

24. I have skills or passions that I think could work as a business.

    a) True

    b) Sometimes true

    c) False

SCORE THE TEST

Look over the questions and then, using the chart on the next page, give yourself the number of points corresponding to the answer you selected. Circle your score for each answer and then add up your points.

FREELANCE ASSESSMENT TEST SCORESHEET

Answer	Points	Answer	Points	Answer	Points	Answer	Points
1a	6	7a	6	13a	6	19a	6
1b	3	7b	3	13b	3	19b	3
1c	0	7c	0	13c	0	19c	0
2a	6	8a	0	14a	6	20a	6
2b	3	8b	3	14b	3	20b	3
2c	0	8c	6	14c	0	20c	0
3a	0	9a	0	15a	0	21a	0
3b	3	9b	3	15b	3	21b	3
3c	6	9c	6	15c	6	21c	6
4a	6	10a	0	16a	6	22a	6
4b	3	10b	3	16b	3	22b	3
4c	0	10c	6	16c	0	22c	0
5a	6	11a	6	17a	6	23a	0
5b	3	11b	3	17b	3	23b	3
5c	0	11c	0	17c	0	23c	6
6a	0	12a	0	18a	0	24a	6
6b	3	12b	3	18b	3	24b	3
6c	6	12c	6	18c	6	24c	0

100–144:   **You're a natural.** You might *already* be freelancing.

72–99:   **It's a good fit.** You may have to make some adjustments, but you're well equipped to handle freelancing.

71–37:   **Caution: This may not work out.** You really need to make some major changes to your habits and beliefs before you can enjoy freelancing, let alone be successful at it.

0–36:   **Stay where you are.** Freelancing will drive you crazy.

How did you score? Do you need to rethink your desire to freelance or are you now more determined that this is the right path to pursue? Even if you scored low, you may want to look back at the areas in which you were strong or weak, and where you can make any adjustments. The following section explains each trait in more detail.

The Necessary Traits

According to insiders, certain traits are absolutely critical to successfully running a freelance business. Various other traits are necessary, but can be learned, or even worked around. Let's go through each one.

ABILITY TO WORK INDEPENDENTLY

Necessity factor: Critical

To succeed as a freelancer, you need to be able to work independently, often without much direction from your clients. Freelancing is not for people who like to wait for their marching orders to begin a project. "Those clichés, like [being a] self-starter, apply here," says one freelancer writer. However, don't confuse "independent" with "loner." While introverts often do very well in freelance careers (many in the creative fields may characterize themselves as introverted), those with terrible social skills—or inflated egos—as a rule do not. "Freelancing is not being cut off from the world," says one freelance illustrator. "Without clients, you don't have a business." (See People and Communication Skills, following.)

STRONG WORK ETHIC

Necessity factor: Critical

Some who've never worked solo might imbue the notion of freelance work with too much emphasis on "free," and not enough on "work." Not so, say freelancers, who add that they work hard—if not harder than some of their counterparts in traditional careers. "Every day I wake up unemployed," says one public relations freelancer. "You need to be ambitious… hungry… thinking about tomorrow. It is certainly not for anyone who is lazy."

Most freelancers, particularly when they're beginning their career, put in close to 60 to 80 hours of work per week. But there's one big difference between doing this for yourself and doing it for a company: It doesn't feel like work. "I work hard—over 80 hours a week.... There's nobody here feeding me grapes," says an actor/writer/inventor. "But I love it.... My work, hobbies, and life really all blend in together."

CONFIDENCE IN SELF AND ABILITIES

Necessity factor: Critical

Confidence in yourself and your abilities cannot be faked. If you have low self-esteem, or continually doubt your talents, you won't have much luck convincing people to hire you. "This is not a good career for people who have self-confidence issues," says one insider. "If there's an easy recipe for self-doubt, it's freelancing—because you can bet you're going to lose clients, regardless of how good you are." One freelance business consultant says that self-confidence is the difference between people like herself and those still in the corporate world who only dream of breaking free: "I'm willing to put myself in front of people.... I'm not easily embarrassed or afraid of making a fool of myself." Says one graphic artist, "Having self-confidence gives your clients confidence.... You need to exude the aura of 'I know what I'm doing and it's worth hiring me for a lot of money to do it.'"

CREATIVITY AND FLEXIBILITY

Necessity factor: Critical

Being creative doesn't mean that you must be in a creative field. It just means that you're able to think outside the cubicle when approaching a project. It means imaginatively approaching your marketing strategies or solving client problems. "You need to not only be creative, but brave in your creativity," says a graphic designer. A business consultant adds, "Part of working freelance is that you have to be able to be creative on the fly… with your projects, people… taking information and going with a new idea. This is a real creative act—no matter what field you're in."

The ability to be flexible in your work life is something that every insider brings up when speaking about his or her career. "You need to be willing to take the ups and downs and not get too stressed out by those low periods," says a graphic designer. "You need to love the fact that every day may be different."

BUSINESS SENSE

Necessity factor: Critical, but can be learned

You may not have a head for business, but not to worry: This is one trait you can learn—provided that you want to learn. Freelancing is not for prima donnas who don't want to do the grunt work. This includes, but is not limited to, bookkeeping, calculating taxes, marketing, handling public relations, and even cleaning. "I take pride in the fact that I clean my own office space," says one financial planner. "If you hire everything out, you won't be making much money."

If you don't have business experience, you have to be willing to learn. "My advice is to take classes at a local college for the skills you are lacking," says one insider. "I had to learn bookkeeping."

ORGANIZATIONAL SKILLS

Necessity factor: Important, but can be learned

Those who think freelancing means you can be loosey-goosey with your time are in for a rude awakening. If nothing else, you need to be more organized than you might have to be in the corporate world, which has a formalized structure in place. If you lack organizational skills, your day-to-day life will be chaotic and unfocused. And you will not make money. While your business will be able to survive if you're not a neat freak—a messy desk, for example, wouldn't be the end of your freelance career—you still need the ability to structure your day so that you can accomplish your tasks and make your deadlines. All of the insiders we interviewed have some kind of time-management system that works for them. Several of them use a "block scheduling" method similar to what students use to organize their days according to classes. Most use an agenda planner or other type of calendar; still others use a giant white board or computer program that alerts them to tasks that need to be done. Time off is scheduled in as well.

PEOPLE AND COMMUNICATION SKILLS

Necessity factor: Critical, but can be learned

Working solo means that you no longer have to be bothered by annoying bosses, nosy coworkers, and disruptive office politics. But you still have to interact with people (your clients) because without them, you will not have work. While you are working alone for a good part of the day (in some professions at least), freelancing is not for cave-dwellers. You do need a good dose of people skills to get clients and keep them. "You really have to love people to freelance," says an animal communicator (see the Real People Profiles section for details on this unique career choice), who needs to communicate well with both her human and animal clients. "You have to be pleasant even when you don't feel like it because that will translate into your bottom line."

If you're weak in this area, consider joining an organization that will help you get out there and start talking to people who may be very different from you—Toastmasters (http://www.toastmasters.org), for example, your local chamber of commerce, or a business networking group. (For an extensive discussion of networking, see the WetFeet Insider Guide *Networking Works!*, available at http://www.wetfeet.com.) Networking can be an unpalatable thought to those who are shy or reserved, but take it from an introverted writer: It gets easier with practice. You'll soon learn that getting out there is not only invaluable to your business, it's also fun.

VISION AND PASSION

Necessity factor: Without this, you're sunk

Working for yourself is vastly different than working for a company in that you must have vision in order to sustain your enthusiasm. Without it, you'll never be able to convince someone to hire you. "You really have to love what you're doing because sometimes it can be a gigantic pain in the ass," says one freelance insider. "But if it's something that you really believe in, you don't mind all those hours you put in."

While you may possess all of the right traits, you won't find any substitutes for raw passion and talent. "You have to really love what you do, and you have to be good at it," says a freelance writer. "That is what will keep you going and get you through the rough spots."

Insider Scoop

WHAT FREELANCERS REALLY LIKE

Free at Last

Although you don't have 100 percent unfettered freedom, the thing most insiders love best about freelancing is the independence that comes with being your own boss. "I create my own life every day," says one freelance writer. Freelancers also shape their own careers every day—and sometimes change course in midstream. For example, over the years I've changed from writing about investments (ho hum) to agricultural writing (interesting), to writing about parenting and New England lifestyles (even better). This freedom to sculpt your career as you see fit is impossible if you're working for someone else—unless you want to job-hop continuously.

Yoga, Walking the Dog, and Taking Fridays Off

Going freelance allows for a lot more flexibility in your day-to-day life. From being there when the kids are sick to having more vacation time, you have the ability to set your own schedule and work when you're most productive. This flexibility works for insiders in a variety of ways. "I like being able to take time off when I want to," says a life coach who works four days a week and takes every Friday off. "We're free to travel," says another insider who recently took his wife and children to England for a month. Says a freelance writer, "I can spend time with my dogs… go shopping in the afternoon." Another freelancer says: "I love being able to exercise in the mornings and go into work late."

It's Not *Groundhog Day*

The fact that every day brings different work and new challenges is a thrill for many insiders. "No two days are the same. I get up at different times. Each day is full of different meanings, different projects," says one insider. "I would get bored if I had to do the same thing over and over," says another.

Home Sweet Home

According to one public relations consultant, being at home has many advantages. "I love being able to conference call while I'm in the kitchen cooking," she says. Attire is also a top reason some love to work at home. "I can work in my pj's now. I don't have to be out the door at a certain time looking radiant, which some days was quite a challenge." says an insider.

Calling the Shots

Insiders love not having to answer to someone in a corner office. And they truly enjoy the fact that if they have a difficult client they always have the option of just "drop-kicking them," as one freelance public relations consultants puts it. "I love being in control of my destiny. I know that every day I have to go out and find work, but that's a more desirable place for me than working for someone else," says an insider. "I choose my own clients. If I were in an agency and a client was paying $10,000 a month and was a jerk, I'd have to do everything possible to make that client happy. Now I can say, 'This is not working out.' And I've done that." Says another, "I love not having a boss. I can say that going to the gym in the middle of the day is a priority for me, but an employer may not understand that." And when things go wrong, some insiders even like the fact that they'll be the only one to blame. "I like that even when I mess up, it's all mine. There's nobody telling me I'm wrong before I even start," said one insider.

WATCH OUT!

Playing Bill Collector

One of the top complaints of many freelancers is having to play every conceivable role in the business. Says one freelance illustrator, "Making calls, filling out invoices—that detracts from what I love about my work." But what most insiders *really* hate is the bill collector role. "The worst thing is when I encounter a client who is slow-paying," says one insider. "I hate chasing the money. I'm not in this to be a collection agency."

Cash Flow—Fits and Starts

Freelancing requires a tolerance for wild fluctuations in your pay, but many insiders still get edgy waiting for the checks to roll in. "I hate it when I'm expecting checks and they're not in yet. And I don't like keeping track of 20 to 30 paychecks a month," says a freelance writer. "I can get four to five months' worth of income in one month and then have some months when no money is coming in," says a business consultant. This can wreak havoc on not only your bank account, but also your sense of self-worth, says an actor/writer: "You can easily attach your self-esteem [to how much money you make]. When you have a fluctuating annual salary, it's tough to get banks to take you seriously. It's tough to get a mortgage," he said.

The Great Client Chase

Keeping client flow steady is the bane of many a freelancer's existence. When work is plentiful, it's hard to think about, let alone do any, marketing. But as a freelancer, you have to sustain your marketing efforts at all times. "I always have to keep my pipeline filled," says a life coach. "I can never fully relax." Says a virtual assistant, "I hate that I worry about where the client base is coming from." Along with the freedom to choose your clients and projects comes the necessity of going out and finding them.

One is the Loneliest Number

Not many insiders miss the corporate life, but some express a vague nostalgia for the friendships and camaraderie of working for a company. "I don't miss it enough to want to go back, but I do miss it from time to time," says one public relations consultant. Another insider says, "Sometimes I hate that it's only me."

Assessing Your Value

Asking for money for your work and accurately valuing the time spent on that work is a challenge for newer freelancers. "This takes confidence," says a graphic designer, who adds that confidence is usually acquired with experience. "I'm getting much better at it," says one insider who's been in business for three years.

Choosing the Right Freelance Career

The Right Reasons to Go Freelance

What's Your Passion?

Putting Your Passions to Work

Careers Suited to Freelancing

The Right Reasons to Go Freelance

Now that you've taken the test and know that you're cut out for freelancing, take some time to think about how you want your freelance life to shape up and what you'd like to do. It's not just a simple matter of picking something that looks good on paper that you can do in your home office for a few hours a day. When you're on your own, the key to success is picking a career that you love. If you're not passionate about what you do, your days will seem as long and tedious as when you worked for someone else.

First, you need to envision the details of your freelance life. Check all of the answers that apply to you.

WHY GO FREELANCE?

Why do you want to start a freelance business?

__I want to stay in my field, but do it solo.

__I'm burned out and want an entirely new career.

__I have a hobby that I love and want to do it for a living.

__I've had it with the corporate world and want out.

__I have kids and want to be home with them.

__My kids are grown and I want a career that I love.

__I'm retired and now want a career that I love.

What's your financial situation?

__I need to work full-time to make money to support myself and my family.

__I need to supplement my spouse's income.

__I want money so I can retire early.

__I want money so I can have freedom to travel (or other activity).

What kind of hours will you work?

__I have to work full-time.

__I need flexible hours.

__I can work part-time.

__I need to work between the hours of _____ and _____ only.

Keep the preceding checklist handy. It's your road map for the remainder of this chapter. While you may find something you're passionate about, if it doesn't meet the criteria you selected, you may not be able to translate that passion into a career that will pay the bills. We'll get back to this later.

First, ask yourself a critical question: *Why* do you want to start a (fill in the blank) freelancing business? Is it just something that seems like a good idea because it's a hot field right now? Is it that a friend or an acquaintance is involved in this kind of work and loves it so much that you think it will be perfect for you, too? Or have you read stories on the Internet that people are making a ton of money doing similar work? Maybe you've dabbled in this kind of business and you think you could do it every day?

While none of these reasons for going solo is necessarily *wrong*, there's one key element that's missing: passion. Insiders cannot stress enough that you should never choose a business because someone else is making money at it. A burning desire to get rich may motivate you for a while, but it's not enough to get you through the hard times. Want to succeed? Pick something you love to do. It's that simple. Your passion and enthusiasm for your work have the magical effect of spilling over into everything you do— every contact you have with a potential customer, every sales letter you write, the website you create for your business. You'll have a better chance of succeeding if you're passionate about what you do. In fact, some say, you really can't go wrong.

What's Your Passion?

Some people can name their passion without hesitation and easily turn it into something that can earn them a living. For others, it takes a little digging. You may have been so busy earning a living in the corporate world or raising a family (or both) that you have not had time to nurture your passions, your hobbies, the things you love.

How can you unearth those buried passions? Here are some exercises to help you do some digging. Don't get put off by the New Age feel to some of these questions. Give them a try. They will help you think and feel your way back to the things you love. Every moment you spend pondering what brings you joy takes you a step closer to a freelance career that will ultimately bring you a wealth of personal (and potentially monetary) satisfaction.

Take some time in a quiet room—give yourself an hour or more—to contemplate and answer (as honestly as you can) the following questions:

 IDENTIFYING YOUR PASSIONS

1. Think back to when you were about eight years old. What did you want to be when you grew up? (It could have been several occupations; list them all.)

_____

_____

_____

_____

_____

IDENTIFYING YOUR PASSIONS, CONT'D

2. Was there anything you loved to do as a child? (Draw? Train dogs? Build model airplanes? Write?)

_____

_____

_____

_____

_____

3. List five things you are good at as an adult.

_____

_____

_____

_____

_____

4. List five things you love to do.

_____

_____

_____

_____

_____

IDENTIFYING YOUR PASSIONS

5.   Imagine that a doctor told you that you have only one hour to live. What would you regret the most in your life?

_____

_____

_____

_____

_____

6.   Do you have an interest or hobby that you're a bit embarrassed about because it seems silly or immature? What is it?

_____

_____

_____

_____

_____

7.   What would you do if you knew you could never fail?

_____

_____

_____

_____

_____

IDENTIFYING YOUR PASSIONS, CONT'D

8. What would you do every day if you were a billionaire?

_____

_____

_____

_____

_____

9. What's your fantasy life like—those daydreams when you're alone in your car, taking a walk, or in the shower?

_____

_____

_____

_____

_____

10. Is there something that you're so skilled at or passionate about that you could easily teach it to others?

_____

_____

_____

_____

_____

Did you find a recurring theme when you did this exercise? Did any interests, hobbies, or passions appear more than three times? Write these down on index cards. Carry them around with you for a week. Look at these themes, whether they be "writer" or "artist" or "farmer" or all three. Don't think about how you will make a living right now. Just start by calling yourself, for example, an artist; see how that feels in your life. Does it feel right? Does it make you happy? Does it make you get up in the morning with a spring in your step? If it does, you've found your passion.

If you need more help in your self-discovery mission, see the For Your Reference section at the back of this book for links to free online self-assessment tools.

Putting Your Passions to Work

Translating what you love into a viable business is a creative and soul-searching process. However, you can't live on love alone, and simply having a passion certainly won't pay your mortgage. But then again, with some creative thinking, it just might.

Let's say that you love to make origami—but can you make a living at it? At first blush, it sounds so impractical and silly. But viewed from another angle you'll see that there are many avenues down which origami can take you. You could teach a class about it, write a how-to book or set of articles, give workshops, or even make origami-themed jewelry or home décor (I know someone who does this as a side business). Consider your skills and passions, and brainstorm ways in which you might make a living around them.

More than 14,000 types of jobs are listed in the U.S. Department of Labor's *Dictionary of Occupational Titles*. This makes for a dizzying array of possible freelance career choices. To help simplify things, here's a breakdown of five general skill categories and examples of freelance careers for which they're suitable: Creative, Business, Physical/Outdoors, People, and Special Interest.

Don't worry if none of these career choices suits you. You really can develop a freelance business in almost any line of work as long as you're truly passionate about what you're doing.

Careers Suited to Freelancing

CREATIVE SKILLS

Do you have a creative flair? This category is for writers, visual artists, and those with expressive (acting) talents.

Visual

- Cartoonist
- Creative director
- Corporate or portrait photographer
- Desktop publisher
- Fashion designer
- Graphic designer
- Greeting card designer
- Illustrator
- Interior decorator
- PowerPoint artist
- Video game artist
- Video producer
- Web animator
- Website designer

Written

- Business plan writer
- Copyeditor
- Editor
- Ghostwriter
- Grant writer
- Journalist
- Newsletter writer
- Public relations consultant/writer
- Speech writer
- Technical writer
- Textbook author
- Website content writer

Expressive

- Actor
- Composer
- Clown-for-hire
- Dance instructor
- Music teacher
- Musician
- Party entertainer
- Set/costume designer

Special Considerations

Don't think that just because you are the "creative type" you can avoid contact with people: Clients are your lifeblood. This is the area people associate with freelancers, and it's usually familiar territory for clients. Freelancers in the creative fields usually do well when the economy slips; layoffs may mean that public relations and advertising jobs are cut (they are often the first to go), and companies know that there's a pool of freelancers available for these jobs. The downside to this, of course, is that when companies cut these jobs these creative types will most likely turn to freelancing themselves to tide them over until they find another job—or permanently, which means stiffer competition for the same amount of work. Make sure you have at least five years of experience and a strong portfolio (an online portfolio of your work or clips is invaluable) before you go solo.

Those in the creative fields, particularly in design work and writing, often require large blocks of quiet time alone. So you need to set up a space to make this possible. Setting up a home office for graphic design work may require a higher startup fee than for other occupations because it calls for sophisticated software programs, such as Adobe Illustrator, Photoshop, or Quark, and powerful computers that can handle large amounts of data. A high-quality printer is also a must, and most graphic designers also use a larger-than-average computer screen.

Writing and editing are the most traditional freelance occupations and probably require the least amount of equipment for setting up a home office. All you really need is a computer with a word processing program, an Internet connection, email, and lots of ideas, and you're in business.

Typical Hours

Many people in this field have set business hours since their clients are on the business world time clock. You can, however, work around this. Those in creative fields, in particular, can do the "business" part of their work from 9 to 5, and the "creative" part (writing, drawing, etc.) at night. Demand in these areas is usually high year-round, although advertising and public relations work traditionally slows down in August and December.

Employment Outlook

There are more freelancers in the creative fields than any other, so competition is stiff. You have to be good at what you do and aggressive in finding work if you want to survive. It also helps to find a niche market in which to specialize.

Graphic design is the fastest-growing segment of this category because of the still-expanding Web market and the boom in the video-entertainment market. Increased demand is expected for interior designers from homeowners, offices, and retail establishments as well as a growing number of eldercare institutions (nursing homes, long-term care, etc.).

Opportunities for freelance public relations consultants are also growing as companies are increasingly dissolving their in-house PR staff and outsourcing that work to contractors. There will be an increased need for writers with an expertise in specialty areas, such as law, medicine, technology, science, and economics. Technical writers are also in luck in this rapidly changing high-tech climate with a greater need for writers to churn out user guides, instructional manuals, and training material. However, turnover is high among freelance writers, many of whom leave this lifestyle to go back into the traditional workforce because they can't earn enough on their own.

Visual Arts Associations

American Association of Webmasters (http://www.aawebmasters.com)
American Institute of Graphic Arts (http://www.aiga.org)
Graphic Artists Guild (http://www.gag.org)
International Freelance Photographers Association (http://www.aipress.com)
International Interior Design Association (http://www.iida.org)

Professional Photographers of America (http://www.ppa.com)

Regional Professional Videographer Associations (http://www.videographer.com)

Society of Illustrators (http://www.societyillustrators.org)

The Drawing Board for Illustrators (http://members.aol.com/thedrawing)

Wedding and Event Videographers Association (http://www.weva.com)

Expressive Arts Associations

American Alliance for Health, Physical Education, Recreation and Dance (http://www.aahperd.org)

Actors Equity Association (http://www.actorsequity.org)

American Dance Therapy Association (http://www.adta.org)

American Music Therapy Association (http://www.musictherapy.org)

Clowns of American International (http://www.coai.org)

Music Teachers National Association (http://www.mtna.org)

National Association for Music Education (http://www.menc.org)

National Dance Association (http://www.aahperd.org/nda)

National Dance Teachers Association (http://nationaldanceteachers.org)

World Clown Association (http://www.worldclownassociation.com)

Writing Associations

American Society of Journalists and Authors (http://www.asja.org)

Association of Personal Historians (http://www.personalhistorians.org)

Authors Guild (http://www.authorsguild.org)

Editorial Freelancers Association (http://www.the-efa.org)

National Resume Writers Association (http://www.nrwaweb.com)

National Writers Union (http://www.nwu.org)

Public Relations Society of America (http://www.prsa.org)

Society of American Business Editors & Writers (http://www.sabew.org)

Society for Technical Communication (http://www.stc.org)

BUSINESS SKILLS

Do you love the business environment? You can make a good living working with, organizing, supporting, and helping the business world in a number of ways.

Business Support

- Executive recruiter
- Image consultant
- Life/business coach
- Medical transcriber
- Paralegal
- Speaking coach
- Tradeshow assistant
- Virtual assistant

Sales and Marketing

- Brand strategist
- Market researcher
- Marketing consultant
- Media buyer
- Sales representative
- Web promoter

Organizational

- Business mediator
- Business strategy consultant
- Conference/event planner
- Human resources consultant
- Management consultant
- Media planner
- Professional organizer
- Project management consultant

Financial

- Accountant (audit, forensic, internal, management, tax)
- Art appraiser
- Auctioneer
- Bail bond broker
- Bill collector
- Bookkeeper
- Collections
- Fundraiser
- Investment consultant
- Payroll service
- Securities trader
- Stockbroker
- Tax preparation consultant

Technical

- CD, DVD, or tape duplication
- Computer consultant
- Computer data recovery/ backup services
- Computer disk duplicating services
- Computer instructor
- Computer programmer
- Computer repair
- Computer upgrade services
- Database consultant
- Image scanning services
- Website maintenance

Special Considerations

Freelancing provides a broad range of opportunities for people who want to work with businesses (rather than with the general public). Clients may think of these as areas they outsource to vendors, or for which they hire consultants, rather than freelancers. You may want to use this terminology when approaching clients. New careers—such as that of virtual assistant, almost unheard of five years ago—are popping up every day in this sector, which is one of the fastest-growing for home-based businesses. This category also includes consultants who are experts in their respective fields, advising on business strategy, technology, production, logistics, or any other issue involved in running a business.

- The startup costs are minimal: usually just a desk, computer, Internet connection, and marketing materials.

- Another prerequisite is plenty of experience, and contacts, in a particular industry.

- Because much of this kind of work is done face-to-face with individual clients, people skills are paramount, whether you're helping with financial, technical, or business issues.

- Certification, particularly in the financial fields, is helpful, and may count towards your overall startup cost.

Typical Hours

Many freelancers on the business/technical support side hold traditional 9-to-5 business hours, since their business clients are also on this schedule. Some, such as financial planners, may also hold evening hours as a courtesy to clients.

Employment Outlook

According to a Dun & Bradstreet report, 13 million U.S. companies require some kind of bookkeeping, accounting, and tax preparation service, and these businesses spend more than $30 billion each year on different types of management training. Clearly, there's a lot of money to be made if you can offer business services to other companies. However, this field requires solid experience dealing with business owners and managers, as opposed to dealing with the general public. Trust is key. So get yourself good contacts in the business community and project a professional image.

Business Support Associations

American Association for Medical Transcription (http://www.aamt.org)
Association of Image Consultants (http://www.aici.org)
International Virtual Assistants Association (http://www.ivaa.org)
National Association of Executive Recruiters (http://www.naer.org)
National Federation of Paralegal Associations (http://www.paralegals.org)
Worldwide Association of Business Coaches (http://www.wabccoaches.com)

Sales & Marketing Associations

Manufacturer's Agents National Association (http://www.manaonline.org)
Market Research Association (http://www.mra-net.org)
Sales & Marketing & Executives International (http://www.smei.org)

Business Administration Associations

American Management Association (http://www.amanet.org)
Independent Consultants Association (http://www.ica-assn.org)
International Society of Meeting Planners (http://iami.org)
National Association of Professional Organizers (http://www.napo.net)
Society for Human Resource Management (http://www.shrm.org)
Worldwide Associations for Management Consultants
(http://www.mcninet.com/onassociations.html)

Financial Professional Associations

American Institute of Professional Bookkeepers (http://www.aipb.org)

Association of Chartered Accountants (http://www.acaus.org)

Financial Planning Association (http://www.fpanet.org)

National Association of Stockbrokers (http://www.nastockbrokers.com)

National Association of Tax Professionals (http://www.natptax.com)

Technical Associations

Association of Computer Support Specialists (http://www.acss.org)

Computer Technology Industry Association (http://www.comptia.org)

Independent Computer Consultant Association (http://www.icca.org)

National Association of Computer Consultant Businesses (http://www.naccb.org)

PHYSICAL/OUTDOORS SKILLS

Do you love the great outdoors? Are you a serious athlete? Do you have a green thumb? Check out this category for freelance jobs that suit your skills.

Sports and Travel

- Adventure travel coordinator
- Aerobic instructor
- Fitness camp coordinator/instructor
- Golf coach
- Personal fitness trainer
- River rafting guide
- Scuba diving instructor
- Soccer coach
- Sports marketer
- Survival/navigation instructor
- Tennis coach
- Yoga instructor

Growing, Farming, and Ecology

- Arborist
- Eco-tour operator
- Environmental consultant/planner
- Farm marketing consultant
- Gardener
- Indoor plant care
- Landscape designer
- Organic farmer

Special Considerations

This category is expanding as more people become health-conscious, active, and interested in improving both their indoor and outdoor environments. This area requires a lot of hands-on experience to be successful. You may also be required to obtain certification (particularly if you will be giving instruction) in these fields. The better your qualifications and your testimonials from former clients, the better your chances for success.

Typical Hours

Typical hours for freelancers in the physical and outdoors skills area vary widely. Those who teach may find themselves working nights or weekends when students are available to take classes. Those working outside in agriculture or gardening—depending on where they live—are usually limited to seasonal work.

Employment Outlook

If you're a sports aficionado with a gift for teaching, you may have a shot at a freelance career: 27 percent of coaches and trainers are self-employed and make their living earning cash prizes in their sport, fees for lessons, scouting, or from officiating assignments.

The outlook for travel careers is varied. Opportunities (and commissions) for travel agents are in decline due to an increase in Internet booking. But consumer incomes are rising (albeit slowly) and baby boomers are getting older and becoming more interested in travel; this means that if you have a travel specialty, such as eco-tourism or adventure travel, your chances of starting a business with a healthy demand are good.

Folks with green thumbs will be happy to learn that the opportunities for working in gardening and landscaping are above average, as homeowners don't have a lot of time to do this work themselves. Traditional farming—probably the first "freelance" work-at-home occupation—is expected to continue its decline as family farms struggle with low prices and competition from large corporate farms. Organic farming, however, is a bright spot in agriculture as an increasing number of small-scale farmers have successfully cornered specific markets. Those with both marketing and farming experience may find a unique niche in consulting with farms about agri-tourism, in which farms incorporate tourism with farming, such as running a bed-and-breakfast on a working farm, conducting hayrides, and giving workshops on such topics as cheesemaking and sustainability, both growing movements in farming.

Sports and Travel Associations

Comprehensive list of sporting associations
(http://www.ucalgary.ca/library/ssportsite/assoc.html)
Comprehensive list of travel and trade associations
(http://dmoz.org/Business/Hospitality/Travel/Associations/)

Growing, Farming, and Ecology Associations

Comprehensive list of landscaping associations
(http://www.landscapeweb.net/pro_associations.htm)
List of sustainable agriculture associations
(http://dmoz.org/Science/Agriculture/Sustainable_Agriculture/Organic_Farming/
Associations/)
Other agriculture organizations
(http://www.business.com/directory/agriculture/organizations/)

PEOPLE SKILLS

You no doubt get your energy from being around people and you love to help them. You may already have experience teaching or tutoring.

Fashion, Beauty, and Personal Grooming

- Bridal consultant
- Cosmetologist
- Fashion coordinator
- Hairdresser
- Makeup artist
- Makeover specialist

Personal Assistance, Healthcare, and Teaching

- Adoption facilitator
- After-school shuttle service
- Au pair coordinator
- Child-care provider
- Doula/midwife
- Eldercare companion
- Home schooling consultant
- Life coach
- Massage therapist
- Private investigator
- Professional organizer
- Stress-management consultant
- Tutor
- Wedding planner

Special Considerations

- Since you're working with the general public, you may need actual office space at some point if you don't want a daily parade of clients traipsing through your home.

- Highly refined people skills, including sensitivity, good listening skills, and an ability to establish rapport with clients, are critical.

- Trust is particularly imperative for those working in the personal assistance and health-care fields, as word-of-mouth is invaluable for building your business.

- Most of these careers offer good freelance opportunities with minimal startup costs.

- You can take online courses to receive training in many of these fields, such as life/business coaching or bridal consulting. Others require special degrees or certification.

Typical Hours

Most freelancers in these areas can set 9-to-5 hours, but expect to have evening and weekend appointments as well to accommodate clients who work typical business hours.

Employment Outlook

Because many of these services are considered a luxury, the demand is higher in metropolitan areas. Of the freelance opportunities listed in this category, by far the best bets are in child care and professional organizing, which are expected to grow as the demand for these services increases due to the prevalence of two-paycheck households. Finding creative solutions for busy households may be the best service to provide to families.

Fashion, Beauty, and Personal Grooming Associations

Association of Bridal Consultants (http://www.bridalassn.com)

Association of Certified Professional Wedding Consultants (http://www.acpwc.com)

Personal Assistance, Healthcare, and Teaching Associations

American Association for Homecare (http://www.aahomecare.org)

Doulas of North America (http://www.dona.org)

International Association of Coaches (http://www.internationalassociationofcoaches.org)

International Au-Pair Association (http://www.iapa.org)

International Coach Federation (http://www.coachfederation.org)

National Association of Childcare Resources (http://www.naccrra.net)

National Association of Postpartum Care Services (http://www.napcs.org)

National Association of Professional Organizers (http://www.napo.net)

National Tutoring Association (http://ntatutor.org)

SPECIAL INTEREST SKILLS

Turning your hobby or volunteer work into a career may be the most enjoyable way to become a freelancer.

Animals

- Animal breeder
- Animal communicator
- Aquarium cleaning service
- Dog obedience instructor
- Horseback riding instructor
- Pet groomer
- Pet sitter/walker

Hobbies

- Book binder
- Gardening consultant/instructor
- Ice carver
- Knitting instructor
- Quilting instructor/workshop leader
- Sewing instructor

Food

- Caterer
- Custom wedding cake maker
- Personal chef
- Meal-delivery service

Special Considerations

Most who decide to work solo in this category are already passionate about what they do. Your cooking, animal skills, gardening abilities, knitting, and handyperson skills need to be top-notch or you'll have trouble getting referrals—the lifeblood of these careers. There are many creative options for making money with what probably started as a hobby.

- You can teach workshops, consult, work in people's homes or offices, tutor, and give demonstrations. You need strong marketing skills to be able to come up with ways of earning a living in this area.

- There are also many people who make a profit using online auction sites, such as eBay, to sell their creations.

- Note that many states require special kitchens and licenses for those working in food preparation (such as catering). Check your local regulations for details.

Typical Hours

Although you may have a home office as well, most of your work will probably be done outside your home in a client office or space. Hours will vary according to the availability of your clients.

Employment Outlook

As with other businesses, you'll need to do your homework to learn how to turn your hobby into a viable freelance career; you might benefit from the help of a mentor (online or otherwise) to steer you in the right direction. Beware of possible burnout, particularly since you truly love your hobby now: Turning it into a full-time business may make it something entirely different and not to your liking. The upshot is that this can be the business in which, if you succeed, all your work will seem like play.

Animal Care Associations

American Riding Instructors Association (http://www.riding-instructor.com)
Association of Pet Dog Trainers (http://www.apdt.com)
National Association of Professional Pet Sitters (http://www.petsitters.org)
National Dog Groomers Association (http://www.nationaldoggroomers.com)

Hobby Associations

Craft & Hobby Association (http://www.hobby.org)

Culinary Associations

American Personal Chef Association & Institute (http://www.personalchef.com)
International Caterers Association (http://www.icacater.org)
US Personal Chef Association (http://www.uspca.com)

You have your work cut out for you. Pick a category, winnow down your choices, and do your research. Then compare what you've got against your first checklist. Will your freelance career choice provide for you and your family? Does thinking about going solo with this career make your heart go pitter-patter?

Of course, before you can even think about clearing out your cubicle, you'll need to get your freelance house in order. Read on.

Before You Hang Out Your Shingle

Write a Business Plan

Designate Space and Time

Devise a Billing System

Spread a Safety Net

Drum Up Demand

Establish a Network

Licenses, Government Requirements, and Insurance

Write a Business Plan

Even if you know exactly what you'd like to do, you still need to get certain things in place before you take the plunge. The beauty of freelancing is that you don't have to quit your full-time job right away: You can start a business on the side and be a "toe-dipper" for as long as it takes to get your business to get off the ground. But make sure your moonlighting is okay (or doesn't interfere) with your employer.

The first thing you need to do before you venture out as a freelancer is to write a business plan.

Before your eyes glaze over and you skip to the next section, hold on. Your business plan doesn't have to be a long, involved 100-page document. All you need is a road map—and it can be as abbreviated as you want it to be. The important part of creating a business plan is that it makes you think—*really think*—about where you want your business to go. It doesn't have to be a work of literary prose, either. A nuts-and-bolts plan will suffice, and you'll probably be the only one who sees it (unless, of course, you want to go for a business loan, in which case you'll need a more elaborate and formal business plan. See Additional Resources at the end of this section for help).

This process can be completed over the course of several days if you wish, and expanded as needed. Remember, your business plan is a living document—you can revise until you get it just right.

Here are the basic steps involved in creating a plan that will get your business started on the right foot.

At the top of a blank page entitled "Business Plan," type your name, address, business name (or proposed business name), phone number, email address, and website. Then answer the following questions:

1. **Executive summary:** What is your business all about? Make this a succinct statement—two or three sentences.

2. **Objectives:** What are your concrete objectives? Here's where you put down three to four specific, measurable business objectives; this usually includes how much you want to make per month, or the number of clients you'll need to make your desired annual salary.

3. **Mission statement:** What is the mission for your business? Here's where you define what makes you special. This is not about your objectives, which are more concrete. This is about your values and how you plan to translate your values into a business. Put down what is important to you. Do you value your creativity, but place equal emphasis on the clients' opinion? This is the place to say that.

4. **Services:** What kinds of services will you offer your clients? List and explain them in detail.

5. **Target market:** Who are your potential clients? Seniors? Businesses (small, medium or large)? Students? Nonprofits?

6. **Market potential:** What is the need for your type of business? Who are your competitors? No need to go to a marketing firm for this information. You can dig up quite a lot of it from your local chamber of commerce or through Web searching. Another good way to gather this data is to present your freelance idea to an informal group of friends or colleagues and ask for feedback.

7. **Marketing plan:** What is your marketing strategy? How do you plan to get the word out about your business? Brochures? Press releases? Word of mouth? Networking? A website?

8. **Financial plan:** How much startup money do you need? What will you charge clients? What kind of equipment and materials do you need to purchase? How much savings do you have as a cushion? Do you have a spouse who can provide a steady income while you get your business off the ground?

Once you answer these questions, you're more than halfway to creating a full-fledged business plan. You can download templates for a formal business plan at the SCORE website (along with other helpful financial and accounting statements) at http://www. score.org/template_gallery.html.

For a free, questionnaire-style mini-plan, visit the *Wall Street Journal*'s startup page at http://wsj.miniplan.com (a short registration is required).

Remember, there is a direct correlation between planning and success. Don't try to wing it without a business plan. Every business can benefit from a plan—even a one-person freelance operation. Just the process of making your plan will organize your thoughts and help you focus, both keys to success in the freelance world.

Designate Space and Time

Do you have a space in which to work? It doesn't have to be elaborate (at least at first). It just needs to be quiet and away from the hubbub of the household traffic. Carve out a space (*not* on the kitchen table or on your bed) for a desk, computer, printer, and phone. A private space—preferably with a door to shut out unwanted distractions—is the best option. At the very least, try to set up a screen or curtain as an important visual divider between work and domestic life.

When creating your work space, make sure that everything is within reach so you're not getting up every two minutes to get something (such as your files, phone, keyboard). It's also helpful to get some mobile equipment, such as a laptop and a cell phone, for those times you want to work elsewhere (like in your backyard or at the beach). Another idea worth its weight in chiropractors' and optometrists' fees is to have a good chair and good lighting. Both will help your productivity and ward off fatigue.

Set your work hours to distinguish between time for work and time for your domestic or social life. Designate a time to start work every day, or each week, depending on how much time you plan to devote to your freelance business, and stick to it. Your work hours should be based on the times of day that you feel most productive. Go ahead and be lulled during your afternoon lull, but make sure you can make up that time later when you're more alert. Make sure your family members (or roommates or whomever you share a living space with) understand that they are not to disturb you when you are working. (Of course, being able to make time for loved ones in special circumstances is part of the beauty of being self-employed.) Oh yes, and be prepared to regularly put in more than a typical eight-hour day.

Devise a Billing System

The way in which freelancers charge for their work varies widely for each profession (and even within professions). Some freelancers want clients to sign written contracts, while others are fine with a handshake. Some provide their clients written estimates and request deposits. Others just do the work and bill the client at the end of the assignment. Whatever your preference may be, make sure you keep copies of all contracts and invoices and keep a log of your receipts so you know if you've been paid. Also, ask your clients if they prefer an invoice sent via email or regular mail.

Freelancers also measure their time in different ways. Some charge by the day or hour while others charge on a project basis and work under a contract. It all depends on the client and the project.

SAMPLE INVOICE

DATE: (Date invoice is sent)

TO:
Joe Schmoe
Schmoe Shoes
1234 Sole Street
Walker City, Middlestate, 95555
(800) 555-5555
Joe@schmoeshoes.com

FROM:
Jill Schill
1234 Freelance Highway
Freedom City, Metrostate, 94444
(800) 555-1234
you@successfulfreelancer.com

Copyediting, 10 hours @ $50/hr...................................... $500.00
Revisions, 2 hours @ $50/hr.. $100.00

TOTAL DUE...$600.00

PAYABLE UPON RECEIPT*
[You can add any special notes here, such as to whom the check should be made payable or your Paypal address].

Thank you,
Jill Schill

*Note: I've begun adding this line to encourage more timely payments from clients. Remember, you're a business, just like your electric or gas company—if they won't tolerate customers paying bills three months late, neither should you. If you'd like to give your clients some leeway, you can instead go with "NET 15" or "NET 30," meaning payable within 15 or 30 days, respectively.

WORKING WITH CONTRACTS

Many situations are better suited to working with a contract. One rule of thumb is to keep large projects (those requiring more than 30 hours of work) on contract, since they will take up a lot of your time and you may be putting other work aside to get them done. Working with a contract also gives you more options for payment. You can negotiate for up-front fees (one third or half of the cost of the project) to help with your cash flow (important for projects that take weeks to complete).

Presenting a Proposal

When working with a contract and estimating the full project fee, start with a proposal to ensure that your expectations and your client's are fully aligned.

A work proposal doesn't have to be long and involved. Here are some guidelines for preparing one.

1. Include your name, date, client's name, and a paragraph explaining the purpose and scope of the project.

2. Prepare an estimate of your time (and cost) for each major step of the project (see the following section for tips on estimating your fees), including any materials. If/when you encounter delays, make sure to note that any additional time or materials needed to complete it will be charged back to the client. Be firm about this or you will end up working for next to nothing if you get a client who can't make up his or her mind. And keep all of your receipts associated with the project costs.

3. Ask for half, or one third, of the project fee up front. State that you'll collect the remaining balance upon completion of the project.

4. Give an estimated completion date—a deadline.

5. Provide a line for the client's signature—and yours. Make two copies and give the client one. Keep the other for your records.

VALUING YOUR TIME

If you're uncertain what to charge on an hourly basis for your work, one good way to figure out how other freelancers in your profession handle billing is to make friendly contact with freelancers *outside your market area* who are working in a city or town similar in size to the one in which you live. Find names on the Web and contact them by phone or email. You may feel a little sneaky or strange doing this, but it isn't sneaky at all. Just be up front about what you're doing—you're starting up a new business and need help and advice. Make sure you point out that you're working in a different community and won't be overlapping clients. You'll be amazed at the positive response (and support) you get. I tried this when starting up my personal history business with good results, and I often have freelancers contact me about my writing fees and how I operate. It's flattering to be asked for advice, so don't assume that you're imposing. The worst they can say is they don't want to reveal that information.

You can also try to check out your profession's trade associations, which often collect and publish pricing data. This information can be found online. (Check the "What is Your Passion?" and "For Your Reference" sections for online resources.)

You can also figure out your rate based on what you need to make to survive (and thrive) and see if this falls into a realistic range. The Council for Community Economic Research (ACCRA) provides an online tool to help you calculate the cost of living in your area, and compare it nationwide (http://www.coli.org/).

The finesse, of course, comes from knowing how long it will take you to complete a particular project. Your labor costs must take into account every aspect of the project

CALCULATING HOURLY RATES

One tried-and-true method to estimate a reasonable hourly rate is this simple calculation:

$$\frac{\textbf{Salary + Overhead + Profit}}{\textbf{Billable Hours}} = \textbf{Hourly Rate}$$

1. Figure out what you want to make per year. This could be the salary you earned at your traditional job, or what you know you need to earn to pay your bills. Let's say this number is **$50,000**.

2. Figuring out your overhead is trickier—rather difficult if you haven't started your business yet, but try to make an intelligent guess. You probably already have a computer and printer at home, maybe even a desk. Now what about paper, ink cartridges, Internet service, extra utilities you'll be using by being at home, advertising costs, any educational costs, and self-employment tax? For simplicity's sake, let's say this all adds up to **$10,000** a year. (Remember, all, or a good percentage, of your expenses are tax deductible).

3. Now what will your profit be—the money left over after paying yourself and paying the bills? It's your bonus. It can be put back into the business to expand into new markets, buy new equipment, or whatever it takes to make your business stronger. Give yourself **$20,000**.

4. Next, figure out how many hours you can bill your clients. Remember, even though you may be working 40 hours a week, 50 weeks per year (you're going to take a two-week vacation, right?), you need to account for sick days and other days when you can't (or don't want to) work. You also need to realize that about half your time will be taken up by non-billable hours that are required to run your business, such as marketing, bookkeeping, and finding new business. Let's say, realistically, you can bill 25 hours a week for 48 weeks. That's 1,200 billable hours.

Now let's do the math:

$$\frac{\$50,000 + \$10,000 + \$20,000}{\textbf{1,200 billable hours}} = \textbf{\$66 per hour}$$

CALCULATING PROJECT FEES

If you don't want to charge by the hour, you can use the hourly rate you just calculated as a starting point for figuring out what to charge per day or per project.

Charging by the day is easy. We'll use our hourly rate above for this example:

$66 per hour x 8 hours = $528 per day

Round it off to $550 a day for good measure. Many freelancers such as photographers prefer to charge by the day.

If you want to charge by the project (which some clients prefer so they can budget their costs), you will have to calculate this separately according to the requirements of each project. But the formula is essentially the same as that for a daily rate. You'll need to multiply your hourly rate by the amount of labor you think the project will involve, by the hour or by the day, then add in expenses, such as supplies, rental equipment, or outsourcing:

(Hourly Rate x Number of Hours or Days) + Cost of Expenses = Project Estimate

The standard rule of thumb when launching a business that will serve as your only income source is to have 9 to 12 months of income saved as a cushion.

from start to finish, including research, actual work towards the project's completion, changes made by the client, meetings with the client… everything. This may be hard to figure out when you're just getting started. Make sure you track your expenses carefully and save all receipts to add this to your bill—no nickel-and-diming here, such as charging for paper, but honest costs associated with a particular project, such as printing or telephone charges. When in doubt, estimate high, and then charge low if you don't spend all that you budgeted for. Your clients will think they've got a deal. The reverse often causes hard feelings all around—the lowest number you give your clients (even if it's a range) will be the number that sticks in their heads. They will feel like they're paying too much if you have to tell them the project is going over budget.

Spread a Safety Net

Can you afford to freelance? Again, think about starting your freelance business on the side and keeping your day job so that you're not digging yourself into a financial hole. But check first with your employer's moonlighting policy (if there is one). Many employers don't forbid employees from starting up a business on the side if it doesn't interfere with their work and if there is no conflict of interest (which could be a problem if you are freelancing in the field you are currently in). Be open with your employer if you feel your job will not be in jeopardy in any way. After all, many former employers end up becoming a freelancer's clients. Of course, in some cases, you may find it best to keep your plans to yourself. Assess the situation; only you can decide whether telling your boss is the right thing to do.

You may also want to consider how much money you'll need in reserve before launching into your business full-time. The standard rule of thumb when launching a business that will serve as your only income source is to have 9 to 12 months of income saved as a cushion. In other words, assume the worst—that you won't make any money for up to a year. If you have this money already in the bank, you can focus exclusively on launching your business and building a new income stream.

If you have a spouse working full-time with benefits, you're probably in the best situation, provided you can live on one salary for a while. This may require cutting back on household expenditures. Sit down with your spouse or significant other and do the numbers. "I made practically no money the first year," says one insider, who had a spouse working full-time to help her get her business off the ground. "I made a little money the following year and better money the next year. This meant no vacations for us for a while."

Drum Up Demand

Many people starting up in business don't consider this, but it's a good idea to get the word out about what you do *before* you formally begin. Make sure you have all your ducks in a row, including your business plan, home office, business cards, and pricing structure, so you're not fumbling for answers when the phone starts to ring. "Talk about what you're doing with everyone you know in your community," says one insider. "You'll never know whom you'll run into who will want to hire you." Another insider recommends always carrying your cards with you: "You don't need to be pushy, but if you hear a need, you can whip out your card and say, 'Maybe I can help. Here's my card.'"

Word of mouth, insiders say, is the best way to get business. But getting those first clients (the ones who are in the position to give you word-of-mouth recommendations) is not easy. Here are some tips on getting that first client:

1. **Gather samples of your work to create a portfolio and a resume.** This "pre-startup" period is also a good time to create a website with your credentials and work samples. Make sure your business cards include your website address, and every time you send out an email, include your phone number and website address.

2. **Offer free consultations.** You don't have to give away all of your work—and for goodness' sake, don't start working for free. But offer a little—enough to be helpful. For example, a public relations consultant could offer a complimentary analysis of a company's public relations strategy, or a financial planner could give a free one-hour consultation. This will get you out into the community to establish some relationships, and hopefully get you some paying clients.

3. **Get referrals and testimonials** from people you've worked with or for in the

past. Put the testimonials on your brochure and website. Contact all of your former colleagues and give them your card to tell them about your new business. Don't be afraid to ask if they know anyone who needs your services. Follow up with every lead, even if it seems like a dead end.

> **Talk about what you're doing with everyone you know in your community. You'll never know whom you'll run into who will want to hire you.**

4. **Make yourself an expert.** Offer a free seminar on your area of expertise. This worked particularly well for one financial planner when he began his freelance business: "I had no idea that millionaires would be in the audience. Many of them became my clients." You might consider creating an e-newsletter on your website, with opt-in subscribers (that's the law now), offering tips and advice in your field. This will help establish you as an expert in your field. If you have writing skills, you can write articles about your area of expertise (again, think how-to stories that will provide advice readers can use), and submit them to the many article databases on the Web.

5. **Work at cost for a charity, friend, or relative.** Offer a reduced fee—enough to break even—for certain clients, and then use the project as a showcase of what you can do. Capitalize on the project by taking pictures (to put on your website, of course), or gain testimonials (again, to use in your brochure, on your website, and in other marketing materials).

6. **Toot your own horn.** Whatever you do, make sure the world knows about it. When it comes to news (when you start your business, expand, or win an award), write a press release and email it to your local newspapers and radio stations. No one is going to seek out the news about your business—you have to be your own best PR person. (You can find plenty of advice on the mechanics of writing a press release on the Web. Just do a search for "how to write a press release.")

Establish a Network

Going from a bustling corporate environment to a quiet home office can be either a relief or an absolute culture shock. The key to preparing for this transition is to develop a network *before* you go whole hog. But networking is not limited to business associates. Make sure you tell everyone you know that you're hanging your own shingle. This includes your friends, family, and neighbors. Your best clients often come by way of the people you know.

You will, of course, also want to network within more formal professional or community groups in your area. Start by scanning your local paper for the times and locations these groups meet. Attend as many as you can (many of them have meetings either before or after business hours so you can certainly start attending them before you quit your job). This is an excellent way to gain business referrals and leads.

Going to these meetings, which are attended mainly by entrepreneurs and freelancers, will quickly help you tap into what I like to call the "underground network" of home-based businesses. You'll soon find a host of people out there to turn to for advice (and companionship) when the need arises. Freelancers, I have found, are a very supportive bunch.

Volunteering is another great way to get involved in the community, spread the word about your business, and build your network. A small amount of *pro bono* work can create an exponential amount of good will, which will be very helpful to you in the long term. People who work in nonprofits are known to be avid networkers, so it's worth your time to get into this loop. (Just make sure you're not violating any conflict of interest rules in the organization.)

Also make contact with others in your field, either through email or professional organizations. The friends I've made through my monthly writers group has proven invaluable in terms of professional support and advice. "I do a lot of my networking through email," says one writer. "I also try to establish relationships with people who work with a lot of other people. If someone needs a writer or editor, he or she can make a referral."

It's also worth your time to get involved with community organizations, such as your local Kiwanis and Rotary clubs, as well as your alumni association and any other special interest groups that interest you. Online bulletin boards, forums, and email listservs are also valuable sources of professional contacts. You can make delightful business contacts all over the country (and the world) by networking at online sites such as http://www. jumpcity.com, http://www.tile.net, http://www.ryze.com, http://www.ecademy.com, http://www.linkedin.com, and http://www.meetup.com.

Licenses, Government Requirements, and Insurance

Most at-home freelance businesses are started on a shoestring. Homes these days have all of the necessary components for a home office, such as a phone, computer with Internet connection, email, fax, and maybe even a little space where you can do your work. Surveys show that many self-employed people start their businesses with $5,000 or less—sometimes much less. For many small businesses, this is usually more than enough to make some professional business cards, letterhead, marketing materials such as a brochure, and maybe even a bare-bones website.

LICENSES

Some states require certain professions—such as catering, day-care center management, and psychology—to have licenses. Check with your state for the particulars. You may also need federal licenses or certifications, particularly if you're working in the financial services industry.

Also check with your city or town for any legal steps you need to take before setting up your home office. Pesky things such as zoning laws can put you out of business if you don't comply.

Federally Regulated Industries

As a freelancer, you probably won't need a federal license or permit unless your business activity or product is supervised by a federal agency, such as:

- Public transportation and trucking (Motor Carrier Safety Administration)

- Investment advice (Securities and Exchange Commission)

- Preparation of meat products or production of drugs (Food and Drug Administration)

- Tobacco products, alcohol, and firearms (Bureau of Alcohol, Tobacco and Firearms in the U.S. Treasury Department)

In any of these cases, the best source of advice is your professional association, which can direct you to the right federal agency for licensing.

FEDERAL REQUIREMENTS

Before starting your business, you need to take care of a number of requirements with governmental agencies—from the city to the state to the federal government. These steps aren't really all that hard or time-consuming. But finding out what you need to do varies from state to state and each city can have different regulations. Bottom line: You need to comply or you may be fined. Here's what you have to do at the federal level.

Tax Registrations

Working on your own as a freelancer (with no employees) is much simpler than setting up a full-blown brick-and-mortar business. Your social security number can serve as your Employer Identification Number (EIN), also known as a federal tax identification number, which is used to identify your business to the Internal Revenue Service and other federal agencies responsible for regulating businesses. You'll need to apply for an EIN only if you have employees, if you operate your business as a corporation or partnership (see following), or if your business in any way involves trusts, business income tax returns, estates, nonprofit organizations, or farmers' cooperatives, among others. You will also need an EIN if your business services are taxed (that is, if your state taxes personal services and you have to collect sales taxes from clients).

For a complete questionnaire to determine if you need to apply for an EIN see the IRS website at http://www.irs.gov/businesses/small/article/0,,id=98350,00.html. This page will also allow you to download a PDF on all you need to know about EIN numbers and how to obtain one if you need to. If you're still uncertain, contact your local IRS field office (http://www.irs.gov/localcontacts) or call the IRS Business and Specialty Tax Hotline at 800-829-4933.

Those (Scary) Quarterly Taxes

As if April 15 weren't bad enough, freelancers must go through the agony of forking over big chunks of money to the IRS four times a year. Make sure you get good advice from your accountant when you begin your business so you don't have to pay penalties in April; if you don't pay your estimated taxes each quarter you'll get charged interest and non-payment penalties.

If you earned any income in a given IRS quarter (which end June 15, October 15, January 15, and April 15), you'll owe taxes for that quarter. You'll be paying federal income tax and Social Security and Medicare taxes (known together as self-employment tax). Check with your tax adviser for the current self-employment tax rate (which changes periodically).

Depending on where your business is located, you might also be subject to state and local taxes. In addition to talking with your accountant, you should read IRS Publication 505: Tax Withholding and Estimated Tax (available online at http://www.irs.gov/pub/ irs-pdf/p505.pdf). This publication contains good information on how to estimate your taxes, as well as a worksheet to help you figure out your own taxes step by step, taking expenses into account. If you run into questions, you can call the IRS directly at 800-829-1040, extension 9825 (while you may be put on hold for a few minutes, representatives are extremely helpful and will even go through the form with you).

A CPA or tax adviser can also help you with the worksheet, especially for the first year.

DESIGNATING A BUSINESS TYPE

Sole Proprietorship

You will need to adopt a particular form of business, but as a freelancer you can keep it simple by operating as a sole proprietor. (Other options are a corporation, partnership or limited liability company, which you may want to consider if you decide later to grow your business. See following.) The vast majority of small businesses start out as sole proprietorships. These businesses are owned by one person—the person who does all of the work (i.e., you). As a sole proprietor, you own all of the assets of the business and the profits it generates. But you also take on complete responsibility for any of the liabilities or debts the business incurs. The advantages of declaring yourself a sole proprietor are that it is easy to organize, you have complete control, and you receive all the income. But the downside is that you have responsibility for all the liability and debts (if you're ever sued, your personal assets are on the line). You also could be at a disadvantage in raising funds and may often be limited to using funds from personal savings or consumer loans. And some employee benefits, such as owner's medical insurance premiums, are not directly deductible from business income.

Setting up your proprietorship often does not require registration of the business if you are operating under your own name. If, however, you plan to create a business name under which to operate your company, state laws mandate that you register your trade name (see State Requirements following).

As a sole proprietor, you may need some of the following forms at tax time:

Form 1040: Individual Income Tax Return
Schedule C: Profit or Loss from Business (or Schedule C-EZ)
Schedule SE: Self-Employment Tax
Form 1040-ES: Estimated Tax for Individuals
Form 4562: Depreciation and Amortization
Form 8829: Expenses for Business Use of Your Home

Partnership

Freelancers rarely have "partners." Many freelancers simply refer work to each other informally rather than entering into a partnership form of business to handle an increased workload. But if, for whatever reason, you decide to go into a partnership with another freelancer, you'll need to decide what kind of partnership you want. The three types are:

General partnership. A business in which partners divide responsibility for management and liability, as well as the shares of profit or loss according to what they agree on. Most likely, it will be a 50-50 split, unless you agree on something different.

Limited partnership and partnership with limited liability. This is more complex and formal than a general partnership. In a nutshell, "limited" means that most of the partners have limited liability (depending on how much they invested) as well as limited input regarding management decisions (the partners are usually investors).

Joint venture. This form of business is like a general partnership, but is only for a limited period of time or a single project. If the partners in a joint venture do another project, they will then be recognized as an ongoing partnership and will have to change their status to a general partnership.

Limited Liability Company

Some freelancers do become a limited liability company (LLC), which is a new type of hybrid business structure that all 50 states now allow. The biggest advantage to freelancers is that this business form is designed to give businesses the limited liability of a corporation (so personal assets are protected) and the tax breaks and operational flexibility of a general partnership. One advantage to forming an LLC over becoming incorporated is that you avoid double taxation—that is, paying both corporate tax and individual tax. Remember, each state has different rules governing the formation of a limited liability company. So check with your local state office for further details.

Corporation

Chances are, if you're a freelancer at heart, you don't want to expand your business into a corporation. But just in case, this is what a corporation is all about: It is chartered by the state in which it is headquartered, and is considered by law to be separate and apart from those who own it. A corporation can be taxed; it can be sued; it can enter into contracts. The owners of a corporation are its shareholders. The shareholders elect a board of directors to oversee the major policies and decisions. The corporation has a life of its own and does not dissolve when ownership changes.

STATE REQUIREMENTS

State Business Licenses

You may not be required to get a state license, but it doesn't hurt to check. (And if you do, it certainly will help keep you in business.) Contact your local government offices to see if your particular business requires a state license.

If you're doing business under a name other than your own (i.e., a business name), you may be required by your state to register your name (there's usually a nominal fee).

What's in a Name?

You have two basic choices when it comes to naming your business: You can use your legal name ("Mary Smith, Freelance Writer" or "Smith Writing Services") or you can make up a name. There are pros and cons to each. The advantages of using your own name are obvious: There's no doubt what your business is about and who is doing it. But these names might be long and cumbersome, and you may want to select a snappy name that looks good on your business card and letterhead, is easy to remember, and gives the specific impression that you're trying to create.

However, as soon as you start making up names, such as "Wordsmith Unlimited," you enter the realm of fictitious business names, which all need to be registered with a government agency—sometimes the state, but it can be your county clerk's office. Local and state agencies want to keep track of your business name for a number of good reasons. One reason is to avoid customer confusion. (Think of what it would be like if several companies had the same or similar names in your hometown.) Another reason is to help customers—in case they have a complaint with a particular company and don't know the owner's name.

Without registering your business name, you're in no-man's-land legally—contracts can't be enforced, you probably won't be able to open an account with a bank under that name, and most important, you could be stepping on someone else's territory (if another company has that name registered and finds out you're using it, you'll have to change everything, including all of your marketing materials.) Or your competitors could simply take the name out from under you and register it as their own business name.

One simple way of finding out whether the business name you have in mind is being used is to do a Google search. Another good site is http://www.thomasregister.com, an online resource for industrial information. You might also search the U.S. Patent and Trademark Office's Trademark Electronic Business Center (http://www.uspto.gov/main/trademarks.htm). In addition, you'll need to check with the county clerk's office in your city or the corporate division of your state to see whether the name you picked is already on the list of fictitious or assumed business names. If your fictitious name, or something very similar it, is already in use, you should come up with something else. Then contact your state to find out the forms you need to fill out (and the fees you need to pay) to register your name.

Local Requirements

Check zoning laws at your local planning or zoning board or at city hall to make sure the area in which you live allows home-based businesses to operate. Many local governments require that you obtain a home occupation permit, which usually costs a flat fee or a percentage of annual receipts from your business. If you rent, check with your building's management or the local homeowners association to see if there are any restrictions in your neighborhood.

While all this may seem a bit overwhelming, fear not: Most residential zoning laws have become more lenient as more people opt to work at home; as long as you don't have a lot of traffic coming in and out of your house, you don't put up signs, and you don't negatively affect the quality of your neighborhood in any way, you are usually safe. But do check first for your own peace of mind.

Finally, if you're confused about who to contact for any aspect of your business, go to your local chamber of commerce, your trade association, your local chapter of the Small Business Association (SBA), or the Service Corps of Retired Executives (SCORE) to point you in the right direction.

INSURANCE

If you own a home, check your homeowner's policy to see whether the equipment and supplies you'll be using for your business are covered. If not, you may need to purchase some extra insurance to cover your business.

If you rent, check your lease carefully or ask your landlord if you can legally run a business from the rented apartment or house. There may be insurance liability if you have clients come to your home office.

Health insurance is a major concern for freelancers who don't have a spouse or domestic partner with a steady job that includes benefits. The good news is that self-employed health insurance deductions are now 100 percent (up from 70 percent several years ago), so you will be able to deduct all your health premiums.

Now that you know what to do before you launch your freelance business, you'll want to get familiar with—and, therefore, avoid—the potential pitfalls that come with going it alone.

The Potential Pitfalls of Freelancing

So Many Hats—So Little Time

Endless Distractions

The Time Monster

The Home-Office Tango

Workaholics Anonymous

Home Alone

Staying Motivated

So Many Hats—
So Little Time

Freelancing has a dark side that can challenge even the fiercest of lone wolves. You may have to do everything yourself. You may sink into a financial hole. You may whittle away your time and never get anything done. You may work until midnight for weeks on end. And you may find yourself getting lonely, working in the solitude of your home.

But it doesn't have to be this way.

The good news is that you're the boss, head honcho, and CEO. But with this title comes the added responsibility of wearing all of the hats in your business, including that of marketing manager, bookkeeper, communications manager, IT director, secretary, spokesperson, salesperson, and cleaning crew.

The key to maintaining your sanity is prioritization. Rank your tasks according to importance, and outsource what you can without blowing your budget. One business/life coach insider, who makes her living helping small business owners keep everything in balance, suggests identifying the different tasks and treating them all differently. Write down all of your various job descriptions, she says, and "don't let it all blur together. While wearing your bookkeeper hat, stay focused on that and don't switch hats in midstream. It will help you stay on task and get more done."

Consider setting aside one day each week to focus exclusively on administrative or marketing tasks, so that this work is not hanging over your head the rest of the week and you know ahead of time when you'll get it done.

Some, though not many, insiders say they outsource a few tasks. All have at least an accountant and insurance agent. Others benefit from the advice of a lawyer, mentor, or business consultant, and several occasionally hire a virtual assistant to help with administrative tasks. You may consider adding some of the following professionals to your one-person band:

- **Accountant:** To help with taxes, creating a budget, or other financial needs you can't handle yourself.

- **Insurance Agent:** For all kinds of insurance you'll need now that you've broken free of corporate life and all its perks, including but not limited to: health, life, short-term disability, and liability, as well as any extra insurance you need on your home now that you're conducting business there.

- **Lawyer:** To help you determine what kind of licenses or permits you'll need to start up and conduct your business; having a lawyer on hand as a sounding board is also a good idea.

 **INSIDER TIP**

Pace yourself in the beginning—you're running a marathon, not a sprint, and you don't want to burn yourself out early.

- **Adviser/Mentor:** Here's a consultant that won't cost you a dime, and the advice is invaluable. You can find an adviser to help you with encouragement, words of wisdom, and guidance by contacting one of many organizations such as SCORE (http://www.score.org), your local Small Business Development Center (SBDC) (http://www.sba.gov/sbdc), your chamber of commerce, your church or religious institution, or any local university or college.

Endless Distractions

When you work at home, you may find yourself waylaid by a multitude of distractions. It's all too easy to aimlessly surf the Internet, email your friends, spend hours in chat rooms, or run errands. It's also easy to believe (at least initially) that you can do more than just your freelance job, such as run the household or take care of kids, while you're trying to work.

How can you keep on task? Here are a few tried-and-true strategies:

- Have set office hours that you adhere to almost every day.

- Install caller ID, particularly if you don't have a separate phone line for your office. You will usually be able to tell if the call is personal or business-related. If it's personal, let it roll over to your voicemail (another essential service that can be provided by your telephone company at a nominal fee).

- Post a "Do Not Disturb" sign on your office door when you're working. Of course, you can use a different phrase as long as it clearly states that you don't want to be interrupted except in case of an emergency.

- Keep yourself from compulsively checking your email by setting up times to check it, such as first thing in the morning, before or after you eat lunch, and at the end of the day. A good spam filter is also invaluable.

- Take your work seriously and let your friends and neighbors know you're working. A simple "I'm on deadline right now. Can I call you back later?" will suffice.

- Don't do household tasks unless you're taking a short break and the chore has definite parameters. So, by all means, throw in a load of laundry while you're on a tea break. But don't get distracted by the messy laundry room and start an hour-long project organizing your sock drawer.

- By the same token, if you're a parent, don't assume that you'll be able to take care of your kids and work at the same time. While being at home is a blessing for people with children (particularly when school is out or a child is sick), you won't be able to work much without a sitter, particularly if your kids are under the age of five. Sometimes you'll be able to manage, but for the most part, you won't get anything done, causing endless frustration with both your work and your children.

The Time Monster

This troll-like creature sneaks into your day in insidious ways, and before you know it, the day is done and you're not quite sure what you accomplished. The key is to put a leash—in this case, a chart or timetable—on your time to keep on task.

Many insiders talk about "blocking time," or doing projects in chunks, rather than flitting from one task to another. "I have this lovely thing in front of me… that has a bulletin board on one side and huge white board on the other," says an actor/writer. "My schedule is on the white board and it looks like school… you know, English at 10:30, recess at 11:30…. My whole day is clearly laid out."

Many insiders keep a running to-do list. "I work like when I worked at an agency. As I get things done, I check them off my list," says a PR consultant. But when the items on your list all scream at once for your attention, don't freeze like a deer in headlights. Here are a few time-management tips to help you stay organized:

- Get a time-management program that suits you. It could be a portable calendar in which you record your appointments by hand, or a software program that beeps or sends you a message when it's time to start a new project.

- Set goals for yourself every day. Start out the week with overarching five-day goals for your projects. Break these goals down into manageable steps each day.

- Keep a monthly calendar in full view of your workspace. See at a glance all of the projects that are coming due.

- Set up a "no excuses" time schedule where you set your work hours, breaks, and non-work-related activities like exercise, family time, and housework.

- Get organized. Disorganization will cost you time and money. Know offhand where you've stored all of your important documents, client files, CDs, and any other work-related material. Stay on top of your inbox (both electronic and paper) so clutter does not accumulate and overwhelm.

- Give yourself a break. While setting up a time-management structure is good, don't be too rigid. You've left the corporate world behind—remember? A good way to maintain some built-in flexibility is to schedule a floating 30 to 60 minutes a day (maybe broken into five- to ten-minute breaks) when you don't have do anything, except maybe watch the grass grow.

 TIME-MANAGEMENT GOALS

For example: I have several articles to write this week, each in various stages of production.

Five-day goal: By Friday I will finish three articles and send them out to my editor. I will be halfway done with the fourth article. I will start research on two more articles.

Daily goals:

- **Monday:** Interview Ms. X for article on bed-and-breakfasts in Maine. Type up notes for article about elm trees. Research statistics for article on dairy farms.

- **Tuesday:** Interview Mr. Y for bed-and-breakfast article; type up notes and start writing story. Type up research for article on dairy farm and arrange interview with farmer. Arrange interviews for article on elm trees.

Each smaller step will get you closer to completing your goal. Remember to cross off items as you finish them (that's the most satisfying part of keeping a task list).

The Home-Office Tango

Home and work life can easily start to spill over into each other. To start off on the right foot, make sure you set up office hours from the moment you begin your freelancing career. Try to stick with those hours—otherwise, your work may start to bleed into your home life, and soon you'll feel like you're working 'round the clock (see Workaholics Anonymous, following).

This balancing act is a constant struggle that work-at-home freelancers face on a daily basis—even those who have been working at home for many years. "I try to block out my time ahead and try my best not to let one [block] interfere with the other… although I have to admit I'm not that good at it," says a graphic designer who's been working out of her home for ten years.

One solution is to have your office in a physical location that's set apart from the activity of the house. An office with a door (and preferably a lock) is ideal. This isn't always possible, in which case you'll need to put up screens (e.g., if you're in the corner of the living room) and basically create a psychological barrier between work and home life.

If you have trouble separating your work from your home space, try these tips:

- Have separate phone lines for home and business, and get separate email accounts for both.

- Try not to do non-work-related tasks, like paying your home bills, or talking on the phone with friends at your work desk. If necessary, take your mobile phone and go somewhere else in your house.

- When you take a break, step out of your office. Likewise, don't eat lunch at your desk. This will also help prevent burnout. Remember, even if you love your work, you still need a break at various times during the day.

- At the end of the day, shut off your lights, shut down your computer, close your door, and *leave*. If you're in the habit of going into your office at every spare moment of the day, you may be at risk of becoming a workaholic (see following).

Workaholics Anonymous

When you find work that you love, it can sometimes be hard to stay away. Your six- to eight-hour workday begins to stretch into ten to twelve hours… and soon you're working from the moment you wake up until you go to bed. You may even occasionally get up in the middle of the night and sneak in a few more hours. As a result, your personal life suffers, and in turn your business will suffer as well. What you once loved will quickly become the source of your burnout. One way to avoid this is to follow the aforementioned tips on setting clear boundaries between your work and home life. To keep yourself out of Workaholics Anonymous, try some of these tips on for size:

- Don't be available at all times to your clients, and don't send inadvertent signals that you are. Says one consultant, "I make sure I don't send emails to clients at 10 or 11 at night because they will begin to believe I'm available and working at that time. Then they will always expect it."

- Learn to say no. It's hard to say no to work when you don't know when the next paycheck is coming. But learn to turn down projects that don't pay well or require too steep a learning curve to be profitable to you. "I'm learning to say no and make it stick," says one insider. "I'm also learning not to answer my emails over the weekend."

- Don't charge ridiculously low rates. This is a common mistake for those starting out who believe that more business will come their way if they undercut the competition. Yes, you might get more business, but you'll also be working twice as much for half the money, not to mention lowering the market value of your profession. Don't do it.

- Realize that you can't keep going from one huge project to the next without a break. Take a day off. "You can step away from your work for a day without being docked pay," says one insider.

- Keep many irons in the fire. One common way to burn out is to stick with one project over a long period of time. "Boredom can lead to burnout," says one insider.

- Take a day off for yourself. Some freelancers only work four days a week with a three-day weekend—every week. "That's the benefit of working for yourself—to have a 'me' day," says one insider.

- Get rid of some clients. Sometimes you just need to weed out the clients who are giving you a hard time, leading to burnout, or just aren't worth the trouble monetarily. Harsh though it may sound, it's essential that you think of yourself, your energy, and your business.

- Take a nap—as little as ten minutes can get your energy levels up again.

Home Alone

While some like the fact that they're alone all day, others need daily contact with other people. These are the folks who miss those impromptu conversations over the copier, having lunch in the company cafeteria, or taking a coffee break to ask for feedback from colleagues. If you crave contact, you may find yourself obsessively checking email for someone to "talk" to or picking up the phone to make doctors' appointments just to hear someone's voice. As a freelancer, you may be home alone, but you don't have to be lonely. Here are some tips to combat that lonesome feeling:

- Plan your day. Remember the to-do list? It will not only help keep you organized, but will also keep you too busy to notice that you're alone.

- Reach out and touch someone. When you write that to-do list, make sure you include some people time such as networking or having lunch with a friend. At least once every couple of weeks, go to a professional group, club, or business seminar in your community, or attend a trade show.

- Team up with other at-home businesses. Locate other professionals with businesses that are similar to yours and try to meet other freelancers for a cup of coffee. (Believe me, they will enjoy the company as well, and you may even refer business to each other.)

- Get a pet. There's something wonderful about having coworkers who can't talk, but can support you through the hard times with a consoling look. Don't underestimate the power of having pets around to keep you company. A dog in particular will force you to get outside your office (for walks) at least two to three times a day. Cats also make great office companions; they're typically quieter than dogs and require less attention.

- Make friends online. Connect with others in your field through bulletin boards and email exchanges, though you should restrict this activity as online chatting can eat up a lot of your time. This can serve as the virtual water cooler that will help maintain your sanity and provide support when you need it.

- Play some music. If the quiet in your house is driving you to distraction, put on some music. You can also find websites that will give you (free) background sounds while you work. iSerenity (http://www.iserenity.com) offers many soothing background noises, such as wind chimes, rain, a crackling fire, and even city noises for those who miss the urban buzz.

- Give it time. Remember, it's normal to feel lonely when you first start freelancing; it can be a bit of a culture shock to many. But once you build up your client base, you'll be too busy to even notice your surroundings.

Staying Motivated

There comes a point in every freelancer's career when you ask, Why am I doing this? It may be that you're not getting enough work, or that you have too much work, an impossible deadline, or a nightmare client. There's no one else to turn to with this question, which can gnaw away at your motivation.

The key to staying motivated goes back to your passion for the business. This is where those earlier questions about what you love come into play. Remembering why you pursued a freelance career in the first place will help you through the hard and self-doubting times.

It can also be hard to stay motivated when there's no boss leaning over your desk, and no impending bonus, either. Insiders say that the bills landing in their mailboxes are a great motivator. "I want to get paid—that's my biggest driver," says one writer. Most also were driven by deadlines, often imposed by their clients. Others said simply that they love going to work. "It's a rare day that I feel discouraged. That was not the case when I was working for someone else," says one insider.

Still, when you're feeling discouraged, try the following:

- Treat yourself to a reward when you're done with a particular project. Give yourself a day off or indulge in a mid-afternoon movie—you deserve it.

- Set up your office somewhere else for a day. Got your laptop and cell phone? Head to the park, the beach, or some other outdoor setting. Or go to the library or a café. Break up the monotony of being chained to your desk every day.

- Take a break every two hours. Don't sit at your computer for hours on end without a rest period. While you're doing your best to keep your home and office areas separate, there's no rule that you can't leave your office for a while and go "home" to relax, then go back to your office again.

- Protect your personal time. You need to recharge and relax because you are your most valuable asset. Treat yourself that way and respect your need for rest, relaxation, and fun.

READY TO TAKE THE PLUNGE?

By now, you probably have a good idea of what you'd like to do as a newly minted freelancer and the skills you need to turn your vision into a reality, even if you just want to dip your toe in the water. Keep your full-time job until you're confident enough (or have enough freelance work) to hand in your resignation. When you're good and ready, you can plunge in head-first, knowing that you're well-equipped to swim—not sink.

Whatever you decide to do, you can feel good about knowing that you can always fall back on freelancing if you're ever laid off or if you need extra cash.

So what's it really like to work as a freelancer, day in and day out? The next chapter is based on dozens of hours of interviews with freelancers who've been working on their own anywhere from 1 to 22 years; their ages range from 36 to 54. Most work full-time; some work as few as 15 hours a week. Their occupations are diverse, from writing and public relations to acting and illustrating, from animal communicating to video producing.

These freelancers emphasize the fact that they now feel in control of their lives. They seem to embody most—if not all—of the qualities needed for a successful freelance career: confidence, a strong work ethic, talent, and passion. While some say they don't fit the mold of a typical freelancer—"I like security," says one—they are nonetheless able to work around such potential sticking points to create a freelance lifestyle they can thrive in.

Real People Profiles

Writer/Video and Radio Producer

Public Relations Consultant

Financial Planner/Investment Adviser

Public Relations Specialist

Illustrator

Actor/Writer/Film Producer/Inventor

Life and Business Coach

Business Consultant

Virtual Assistant

Animal Communicator

Graphic Designer

Writer/Video and Radio Producer

Age: 40

Years freelancing: ten

Education: Some college, no degree

Hours per week: 30–50

Annual salary range: $50,000–75,000

WHAT DO YOU DO?

I'm a freelance writer, and [I] work in video and radio production. I'm usually working on one to three articles on any given day. I conduct a lot of interviews, mostly by email. Every day I'm identifying people to interview for articles, writing stories, producing TV shows, logging tape, or writing scripts. I work part-time out of my home and part-time out of my RV, where I commute between my home and the TV station that is across the state.

WHAT DID YOU DO BEFORE?

I was in public relations and marketing. I lived in New York City for 13 years and held a variety of jobs there. I started my own Internet company and tried a few other free-lance ventures that flopped. I did take a full-time job for a while and worked in public relations and marketing. I ended up in Wyoming after driving through it and thinking it was the most incredible place. I really made my final decision to move here after September 11.

HOW DID YOU BECOME A FREELANCER?

I started an Internet company that included Web design, hosting, and programming. In the course of my work, I started writing copy for the website, then expanded into writing about the Internet and immediately developed a niche writing about the Internet for women. I ended up writing a few books on the topic and began freelance writing full-time.

WHAT ARE YOUR CAREER ASPIRATIONS?

My husband and I invested in video equipment and started a documentary film company. But there's not a lot of money in [documentary film-making], so I will continue to do freelance writing.

WHAT KINDS OF PEOPLE DO WELL IN FREELANCE CAREERS?

You have to have a high tolerance for the unknown and unexpected. You also have to be creative in terms of earning money and making ends meet. I know so many people who are incredibly smart and talented, but are terrified of not having a guaranteed paycheck.

You need to be constantly marketing, constantly finding jobs.... You can't sit back on your laurels. In the mid-1990s, I had the most amazing freelance writing jobs where I was steadily making $3,000 to $5,000 a month. I sat back, thinking, "This is great." But that was a mistake, because in freelancing you have to assume that nothing lasts forever. Even if you are doing well, you have to constantly seek out new avenues of work. You really have no idea from one day to the next if you'll have work, even when you have steady gigs.

WHAT KINDS OF PEOPLE DON'T DO WELL IN FREELANCING?

Linear thinkers. People who are not risk-takers, who would rather play it safe. People who fear change. I think most people are afraid to take chances. That's why everyone is not a freelancer.

People with more financial burdens often don't go into freelancing. If you own a house, have children, have huge car payments, big medical payments, or don't have a spouse with a steady job… that lends itself to looking for stability.

WHAT DO YOU LOVE ABOUT FREELANCING?

The freedom. I create my own life every day. I love hanging out with my dogs.

I like constant change. I like something new and different every day: new problem to solve, new client to deal with. It is perfectly suited for me. I can go shopping in the morning and have plenty of time during the day or evening to work on or get assignments.

WHAT DO YOU HATE ABOUT IT?

When I'm expecting checks in and they're not in yet. I don't like keeping track of 20 to 30 paychecks a month. Some are $100 and some are $1,500. I don't like being the bill collector—in fact, I'm afraid of doing it. I often do that by email so I don't have to talk to the person. The hard part is negotiating my pay.

WHAT IS THE BIGGEST MISCONCEPTION ABOUT FREELANCING?

That we don't work. That we sit around and don't do anything. I could be running errands all day, and people think I'm not working. But I go home and put in eight to nine hours of work—I just do it at different hours.

LOOKING BACK ON YOUR FREELANCE CAREER, WHAT DO YOU WISH YOU HAD DONE DIFFERENTLY?

I wish I had incorporated sooner. I really think with freelancers there's the tendency not to think of yourself as a business, but you are a business. By incorporating you have to get an accountant and a lawyer—it has not turned out to be the exorbitant fees I thought it would be—and it makes you seem way bigger and more professional. It was not a hassle, and not as expensive as I thought it would be. And the tax breaks are much better.

WHAT ADVICE WOULD YOU GIVE SOMEONE WHO IS LOOKING TO START A FREELANCE CAREER?

Sack away some money on the side. Moonlight if that is not a conflict of interest in your current job. Dabble a little on the side first. Sticking your toe in the water can help you decide. And when your part-time gigs are taking over and can generate enough income, you can safely quit your job.

People should remember that there's real money out there. The question is, what are you willing to do? How much looking around will you do? Because, even in slow times, I have never seen that there isn't money out there.

DAY IN THE LIFE OF A FREELANCE WRITER

6:30 a.m.   Let the dogs out. Have breakfast. Check email.

8:00 a.m.   Yoga class.

9:00 a.m.   Prep my women's business column for *Entrepreneur* magazine. I have three people to interview, including an expert. Compose the questions and email them out to my sources.

10:00 a.m.   Check Writers Market online and file away new market possibilities with magazines.

11:00 a.m.   Work on a query letter for a story idea.

12:00 p.m.   Work on public relations and marketing clients. Write a press release and pitch it to various media.

1:00 p.m.   Take my dogs with me downtown. Eat lunch in the park, then run errands.

3:00 p.m.   Back at my desk. Check email again. Work on a book project.

5:00 p.m.   Review TV show tape. Have dinner at home. Feed the dogs.

6:00 p.m.   Watch back-to-back episodes of *CSI*. That's my vice.

8:00 p.m.   I'm a magazine fanatic. Browse the glossies looking for new markets to write for, read other writers, and find what topics are hot. Do the crossword puzzle.

10:00 p.m.   Go to bed.

Public Relations Consultant

Age: 43
Years freelancing: six
Education: B.S. in journalism, University of Texas
Hours per week: 30
Annual salary range: $50,000–75,000 (charges $100 per hour)

WHAT DO YOU DO?

I'm a public relations consultant. I work on a variety of accounts, including consumer, events, and book authors. Right now I am helping a group from Asia handle publicity for its first U.S. tour. Ninety-nine percent of my business comes from referrals.

WHAT DID YOU DO BEFORE?

I worked for a large, international public relations firm. And before that, I sang in a rock and roll band and toured with them. I always knew I would go to college—this was my dream to be in a band. I decided that by 27, either I would have a recording contract and continue singing or go to college. I ended up going to college.

HOW DID YOU BECOME A FREELANCER?

When I was working for an agency, I was traveling way too much and working way too many hours. I had clients [who] were very difficult, and there was so much pressure. Back then I was a newlywed and I didn't want to spend another anniversary apart from my husband. I was feeling pressure about my home life and business life. I started praying about it—what should I do? I also started talking with people—a banker, a CPA, other freelancers, an attorney, a computer consultant. And I suddenly got calls from former clients who said they couldn't afford the agency rates and they wanted me to do their PR work freelance. I approached my husband, who is a financial planner and doesn't do anything spontaneously. I showed him my plan, my projected income, my hours. He was amazed at the research I had done and that I already had clients lined up. So I did it.

I really put thought into it. And it has been wonderful. I have about five accounts I work on. My work has evolved into more project work instead of retainer work. I write press releases, line up interviews, write pitch letters, write speaking points, help with media interviews, and help develop key messages.

WHAT ARE YOUR CAREER ASPIRATIONS?

I'd like to do a lot more *pro bono* work. No, I will not grow my business. If anything, I would look for an exit strategy. I would like to retire early.

WHAT KIND OF PEOPLE DO WELL IN FREELANCE CAREERS?

People who are driven and who can juggle a lot of responsibility, and those who work well on their own. I'm a very social person, but when it comes to work I'm extremely focused, so I can get more done in four hours at home than two days in an agency.

You also need to be ambitious because when you have plenty of business, it's easy not to continue to look for work. But I know that every day I wake up unemployed, so I have to be hungry and thinking about tomorrow. That is the mindset. Freelancing is certainly not for anyone who is lazy.

You have to be talented. And it helps to be well-connected. I wouldn't encourage someone who's only worked three to five years in business to freelance. Wait until you have seven to ten years under your belt. Because once you get to the level of manager, you'll know what it's like to manage clients, keep a budget. And these are things you will need to run your own business.

WHAT KIND OF PEOPLE DON'T DO WELL IN FREELANCING?

People who have low self-esteem. People who don't work well with others. Some people think that if you work by yourself you don't need to work well with others, but that's not true. On the other hand, you also have to be able to work by yourself without a lot of direction. And people who don't have a lot of experience don't do well in freelancing.

WHAT DO YOU LOVE ABOUT FREELANCING?

I like being the boss of my own destiny. I just know every day, I wake up and I'm unemployed. I've got to go out to find that work. But that's a more desirable place for me than working for someone else.

I love the flexibility. I'm able to schedule things during the day, like working out. I love to cook, so being able to conference call while in the kitchen cooking—I love that. I also just like the ability to work with people I want to work with. When I was working at Edelman, if we had a client paying $10,000 a month and [he] was a jerk, I had to do everything to make that client happy. Now, if I get a client who is rude, I can say: "This is not working for me, but I can refer you to three other people." … And I've done that.

WHAT DO YOU HATE ABOUT IT?

I don't like the administrative aspect. I had a client yesterday who asked me if I had billed him—keeping track of all that is not easy. I also don't like the fact that I'm responsible for all of my equipment and making sure it all works. I also don't like getting inundated with calls—I get graduate students all the time calling me for work. I don't have time—if I had an assistant I could have her handle something like that, but I don't want an assistant. I also get a lot of vendor calls. All of that takes a lot of time away from my work. Sometimes I will outsource, like for building media lists, research for clients, or finding speaking venues, but not often.

WHAT IS THE BIGGEST MISCONCEPTION ABOUT FREELANCING?

If you just go out on your own, you'll get work. That it'll just happen. It doesn't just happen—it takes a lot of work to find work. You should let everybody you know—and whom your spouse knows—that you are freelancing and what you are doing. Get the word out because the work won't fall in your lap.

LOOKING BACK ON YOUR FREELANCE CAREER, WHAT DO YOU WISH YOU HAD DONE DIFFERENTLY?

Nothing, really. Only that I wish I had done it sooner.

WHAT ADVICE WOULD YOU GIVE SOMEONE WHO IS LOOKING TO START A FREELANCE CAREER?

Research the market to find out the demand in your field. Find out how much it will cost you to run a business. Have clients lined up before taking the leap. And, once you start, take it seriously, like a full-time job. When the office phone rings at night, don't answer it. Close your office.

DAY IN THE LIFE OF A FREELANCE PUBLIC RELATIONS CONSULTANT

6:00 a.m.   Have breakfast with my husband and get dressed for work.

7:15 a.m.   Drive to a downtown Dallas hotel and pick up my client for a live TV appearance. (The client is an actor in a theatrical production making its U.S. debut.)

8:00 a.m.   Arrive at the KDFW-TV studio with my client, who is interviewed at 8:30.

9:00 a.m.   Return my client to the hotel.

9:30 a.m.   Return media-related phone calls and emails.

10:00 a.m.   Attend a committee meeting for a nonprofit board on which I serve as president.

12:00 p.m.   Make media follow-up calls for several clients regarding different events, including a theatrical production, a new restaurant opening, and a speaking tour.

12:45 p.m.   Participate in a brainstorm conference call on behalf of a client who is on an 11-city speaking tour.

1:30 p.m.   Change into my workout gear and run for 40 minutes, then bike for 40 minutes. (I'm training for a triathlon in May.)

3:30 p.m.   Draft an activities report for a restaurant client.

4:00 p.m.   Drive to FedEx and overnight B-roll footage (stock footage) to a TV station in another state on behalf of the theatrical production.

4:30 p.m.   Close the office for the weekend.

Note: This day was a little longer due to the live TV appearance that morning. Most days I work from 9 a.m. to 4 p.m., with an hour or two break for workout and lunch.

Financial Planner and Investment Adviser

Age: 54
Years freelancing: 16
Education: B.A. in liberal arts, teaching certificate, MBA
Hours per week: 50–55
Annual salary range: Undisclosed—"I do better than the average MBA."

WHAT DO YOU DO?

I help individuals and families to realize their financial aspirations and goals. I advise them on their investments, retirement accounts, and college savings, and help retirees manage income from their investments.

WHAT DID YOU DO BEFORE?

I was a teacher. I taught in public school for ten years—in elementary and middle school. I've taught all subjects.

HOW DID YOU BECOME A FREELANCER?

I took a year leave of absence after having taught for ten years, due to certain frustrations with the teaching profession. I started exploring my interests and went back to school for my MBA with the idea that I would go into corporate finance. I completed my degree at the beginning of the last recession; this meant all of the job offers [in corporate finance] had dried up. So I found myself fending for myself. I had friends who, knowing I had an MBA, were seeking financial advice from me. One thing led to another and pretty soon I was in business for myself. I have to say that this was not something I dreamed of all my life. It happened by circumstance.

WHAT ARE YOUR CAREER ASPIRATIONS?

Status quo at this point. I don't want to grow my business and add employees—then I would become a business manager instead of financial planner. I don't want to do that.

WHAT KIND OF PEOPLE DO WELL IN FREELANCE CAREERS?

People who are self-directed. You have to be highly motivated and persistent. This didn't happen overnight for me. But when you're in this position, it's sink or swim. I have to say my teaching experience helped me learn to be fairly independent.

WHAT KIND OF PEOPLE DON'T DO WELL IN FREELANCING?

People who are not self-motivated.

WHAT DO YOU LOVE ABOUT FREELANCING?

I like being in the position of making the decisions; the buck starts here. Although I'm in charge, it's the customers who are really in charge. I do have some flexibility—even time-wise. This is something I will be doing until I retire—but I'm not that interested in retiring. I receive a lot of personal satisfaction from this work. My clients feel that they have matured and grown financially. When my clients are happy, that makes me happy. It's pretty simple.

WHAT DO YOU HATE ABOUT IT?

This may sound strange given that the thing I love about freelancing is its flexibility, but inflexibility. Without employees I have no one to delegate to. Sometimes there's a lot of paperwork that needs to get done that goes along with the territory. No, I don't outsource because of the whole confidentiality issue—financial information is very sensitive—regulatory authorities that I have to report to. If I add employees, I will create a web of additional paperwork and costs.

WHAT IS THE BIGGEST MISCONCEPTION ABOUT FREELANCING?

I see these posters on telephone poles that say you can work on your own and make $3,000 a week stuffing envelopes. I don't think people realize how hard it is to work on your own—I suspect I work harder on my own than with an employer. There are not too many Bill Gateses out there who start out in a garage and end up as an empire. I'm not denying there is the occasional person who hits the mother lode, but there are a lot of people who work on their own and barely get by.

LOOKING BACK ON YOUR FREELANCE CAREER, WHAT DO YOU WISH YOU HAD DONE DIFFERENTLY?

I might have early on expanded my education; it would have given me more credentials in the first seven to eight years. Another thing: I don't think I would have moved. I started the business (in another state) and then I moved and that really set me back. It was like starting all over again. If you rely on local business, it's hard to move.

WHAT ADVICE WOULD YOU GIVE SOMEONE WHO IS LOOKING TO START A FREELANCE CAREER?

It takes more than a great idea to succeed. You have to know the business aspect of running your operation. You need to be patient. I overestimated my revenue stream and number of clientele. It was much slower than I thought it would be.

You have to know when to give up or continue. I groveled for about four years… and it finally took off at year five. Other businesses may have a different time frame and it may help to talk to people who are freelancing in your business.

Find out different ways to market yourself—it's not always traditional advertising. For example, I taught evening classes in continuing education at the high school in invest-ments and financial planning. Unbeknownst to me, I'd had millionaires sitting in these classes. I never ran ads or sent out flyers. The school district did the advertising for me—and I didn't treat my classes as a sales pitch. I got a lot of my clients through those classes. I no longer need to teach those classes, because 100 percent of my clients now are word of mouth. I've actually reached full capacity.

DAY IN THE LIFE OF A FREELANCE FINANCIAL PLANNER

6:30 a.m.   Wake up, read professional literature until 8 a.m.

8:00 a.m.   Check email and download online financial data. Send emails to clients regarding business that needs to be addressed. Make several phone calls to clients.

9:15 a.m.   Go out to drop off a package at the post office. Pick up the *Wall Street Journal* and run a personal errand.

10:00 a.m.   Pore over paperwork; analyze data.

10:15 a.m.   Meet with a client for an annual meeting.

12:30 p.m.   Eat lunch and follow that with my daily nap—I have a big couch in my office.

1:00 p.m.   Meet with another client.

3:30 p.m.   Go out in the yard and rake—always have to stay on top of the autumn leaves.

4:00 p.m.   Another client meeting.

6:00 p.m.   Cook dinner with my wife.

7:00 p.m.   Another client meeting—I often have to schedule evening hours to accommodate clients who work full-time.

8:00 p.m.   Done for the day. Spend some more time with my wife before hitting the sack.

Public Relations Specialist

Age: 36

Years freelancing: four

Education: BA in communications and German literature, Cornell University

Hours per week: 30–60

Annual salary range: $100,000+

WHAT DO YOU DO?

I do public relations for high-technology clients, business to business, which means my clients are businesses, rather than individuals. My clients also include a magazine, an investment adviser, and a career counselor.

WHAT DID YOU DO BEFORE?

I wanted to be a reporter. I came into the job market in 1992, which was the time of a pretty bad recession that hit the publishing world hard. I landed a job with a high-tech magazine where I worked as a reporter. But the pay was terrible. I started at $17,000—in New York City it's really hard to pay the rent on that.

I decided to go into public relations because there was more money and opportunity than in journalism. I had the high-tech background because of my work at the magazine. I could have just as easily fallen into advertising. I believe in public relations because it creates a message—a third-party endorsement. That is more believable to me than advertising.

HOW DID YOU BECOME A FREELANCER?

Since my first PR job at an agency, I've dreamed of starting my own agency. Especially when I found out how much my clients at the agency were getting billed, and how much of that I was getting—something like ten percent.

I was doing in-house PR in 2001 for a company that went belly-up. So, I fell into freelancing, even though I wasn't ready to do it and the economy wasn't great. I thought, "Well, let me go out and find a few clients because there are no interesting jobs out there and everybody's offering me half of what I was making." My goal was to take on some clients until I landed the right job. Instead, I picked up one very good client and arranged for a retainer payment to generate something of a steady income.

I then started to pick up more clients. That's when I started to work horrible hours. In hindsight, that was not a very good thing—I was working past midnight every night. But I didn't work on weekends, which was my saving grace.

WHAT ARE YOUR CAREER ASPIRATIONS?

I want to get out of doing this. It's not a freelance thing—it's a PR thing. In the early '90s, PR was ranked the sixth most stressful job in the United States. The problem with working in this business is that you have your demanding clients who don't understand why they're not in the *Wall Street Journal*. Then there's dealing with reporters—even when reporters are very amenable, it becomes a pressure cooker of sorts. I have times when I love it; I have times when I hate it. I have one colleague who has built an agency, with five people working for him, but he's burn[ed out]. You don't see many people in PR [more than] 50 years old.

WHAT KINDS OF PEOPLE DO WELL IN FREELANCE CAREERS?

I used to think that to be successful in freelancing, a person had to be very ambitious and driven. But increasingly, I think the right person for freelancing is someone who is not a nervous hand-wringer type. Someone who can say, "I lost a client that represents 40 percent of my income, but I have enough tucked away for two months." A person like that is not easy to find. It takes someone with a very even temperament. Freelancing is not good for people who have self-confidence issues. If there's an easy recipe for self-doubt, it's freelancing. It's very easy when you lose a client to say, "I'm worthless." Meanwhile, you could have been doing amazing work.

Freelancers need to be people who can roll with the punches and are a little bit hungry. I make more as a freelancer than I ever made with a company.

WHAT KINDS OF PEOPLE DON'T DO WELL IN FREELANCING?

People who are control freaks when it comes to monetary issues. I have clients who have taken three months to pay me. I had a client who decided it wasn't going to pay me, and [I] had to send them a strong letter. Worrywarts would have a hard time in freelancing because, not only do they worry about how much money is coming in, but they also worry if they will lose a client. And over time, that lack of self-confidence shows. A person who is really regimented, who doesn't like surprises, would also have a difficult time with freelancing.

The first time I lost a client, it really ate at me for months. I was so scared that I would lose more clients that I doubled my efforts. But that first experience toughened me, and I don't take it as personally now.

WHAT DO YOU LOVE ABOUT FREELANCING?

I love the overarching benefit of controlling my own destiny. I love not having a boss— I used to have a boss who would nitpick at me when I didn't show up at exactly 9 a.m.—never mind that I was staying at work until 10 p.m. Now I can set my own hours. I can decide that going to the gym is a priority, whereas an employer may not understand that.

I've been able to travel more because I have the time. I pick times to go that will least affect my clients. I take half of August off. And I take the second half of December off as well.

I do like the ability to be able to choose what I want to do. If a client is too difficult to work with, I can always refer them to someone else and graciously bow out.

I can start at 8 a.m. and wrap up at 2 p.m. and have a nice afternoon, and I don't have to explain myself to anyone.

WHAT DO YOU HATE ABOUT IT?

I don't like it when clients aren't happy. I have a real problem with clients who are unreasonable or don't have a terribly interesting story.

From a freelancing perspective, revenue flow is not fun to manage. I don't enjoy the process of invoicing. And I really don't like following up with clients who don't pay their bills.

I also sometimes miss the office camaraderie. I don't miss it enough to want to go back, but I do miss that from time to time.

WHAT IS THE BIGGEST MISCONCEPTION ABOUT FREELANCING?

By far, the fact that you sit back and make money. A lot of people have this concept. Sure, you can make money, but people don't see the three months you spent without income. A lot of people feel freelancing is very easy. But you have a lot of added responsibilities you wouldn't have if you were working for someone else. Such as invoicing and following up on invoices. Having to pay quarterly taxes and find your own healthcare. In a company you're actually paid for your time, so if you go on a new business pitch but don't get the account, you still get paid. As a freelancer, you can spend 30 hours on pitching a new account and still have nothing to show for it. A lot of work goes into getting business, and that's what a lot of people don't realize. That's why freelancers charge more money per hour.

LOOKING BACK ON YOUR FREELANCE CAREER, WHAT DO YOU WISH YOU HAD DONE DIFFERENTLY?

I would have paced myself in the beginning—I should have realized I was running a marathon and not a sprint. It is hard not to be passionate about building something.

WHAT ADVICE WOULD YOU GIVE SOMEONE WHO WANTS TO START A FREELANCE CAREER?

It doesn't matter how much people pay you—you will do the same amount of work for every client. Mentally, the small clients take up as much space as the large clients. So go for the [higher]-paying clients.

And certain professions are better suited to freelancing because they allow you to hit the ground running, such as a service. Get a website and get some clients before setting out on your own.

If you're going to do this right, you should have a comfortable financial cushion in place so that you can allow yourself enough time to get the business going. More important, roll up your sleeves and get out there. Go look for business. You have nothing to lose.

DAY IN THE LIFE OF A PUBLIC RELATIONS CONSULTANT

9:00 a.m.   At my desk, going through email and planning for the day. Usually do phone work in the morning—calling media and pitching stories early in the day, before they get too wrapped up in writing.

10:00 a.m.   Make a cup of tea. It gets me away from my desk, although I come back and review email while the water's boiling. Put on some light background music—lately it's been classical, because it doesn't interfere with phone calls or writing. Then go back to pitching reporters.

12:00 p.m.   Lunchtime. Sometimes I prepare it, but more often my partner does. I'm very lucky. We actually sit down and have lunch together—a very relaxing reprieve.

12:30 p.m.   Back to the grindstone. Now the media pitching goes into full gear before I hit that wall (about 2 or 3 p.m.) when editors do not want phone calls.

2:00 p.m.   Make another cup of tea and put on some more interesting, energetic music—Brazilian as of late. Draft up a press release.

3:30 p.m.   Made another cup of tea. Write a report for a client.

4:30 p.m.   Snack time.

5:00 p.m.   It's the end of the day for many, so it's time for last-minute phone calls.

6:00 p.m.   Now I'm thinking of wrapping up for the day. Lately, I've been coasting into 7 p.m., then watching *Jeopardy* as my end-of-day reward. Then it's off to the gym with dinner after.

Illustrator

Age: 46

Years freelancing: 22

Education: High school diploma; one year college with art major curriculum, but mostly self-taught

Hours per week: Varies; can be up to 12 hours a day, 7 days a week to finish a project; it typically takes five to seven days to finish an average painting; then I take a day or two off; I don't work by a regular calendar

Annual salary range: $75,000–$100,000

WHAT DO YOU DO?

I produce artwork for clients based on their needs, such as paperback book covers, toy designs, motion picture production artwork, or packaging for toys and video games. Most of what I do is science fiction or fantasy-related. I'm a hired creative hand, working under my client's guidelines.

I've done illustration for a mainstream film production company's licensing division. I created artwork for merchandising and licensing companies, which buy licenses to create products branded with a movie's or TV show's images, such as *Star Wars* lunch boxes, and [I] did the covers for some branded comic books. I've been doing the comic books for 13 years now. I've worked with several other large movie production companies' comic book publishers on licensed images; this has built my career. I'm known as the guy who can do licensing very well—this is my niche.

WHAT DID YOU DO BEFORE?

I was very fortunate to have parents who were very supportive of my art and the direction I wanted to go. When I went off to college and didn't find the curriculum I was happy with, I decided to teach myself. I talked to my parents and made arrangements to drop out of college and stay at home with a part-time job to contribute to the household, while working on my craft in my free time. I eventually got to the point where I could get some commercial work. Within two years, I was making a full living.

WHAT ARE YOUR CAREER ASPIRATIONS?

I have a science-fiction spaghetti western project I started. I'm developing it in a number of different venues, through comic book and text novels. I will continue to make time to work on it over the next ten years or so. I want to be able to continue my commercial work to make sure my family is taken care of. But I want more time to explore more fine art painting. I don't see myself retiring. There are a million paintings in my head and there will never be enough time to put all those paintings on canvas.

WHAT KINDS OF PEOPLE DO WELL IN FREELANCE CAREERS?

You need to have patience and persistence because the work won't drop immediately on your lap. It is a lot of work to get yourself known and out there on the marketplace. And if things go well, clients will contact you. Art schools do not teach the business end of art. If you're in this business, you need to understand that painting is one thing, but selling the paintings and making money—that's business. A lot of things that go along with that—tax forms, following up on emails—isn't the fun stuff, but it still needs to be done. I can create the greatest painting in the world, but if I'm not out there promoting myself, I'll be nothing.

You also need to know how to organize a business. There are the odd exceptions who have the talent and a business sense. But most artists fail because they can't keep up with the business end of things.

WHAT KINDS OF PEOPLE DON'T DO WELL IN FREELANCING?

Someone who thinks his art is above his client. This business is all about pleasing your client and knowing the artwork is for them first because they are paying you—even though you also have to like the piece as well.

WHAT DO YOU LOVE ABOUT FREELANCING?

There's a freedom involved in working for myself—as long as I can deliver the work on time I can structure my time as I want. I can go to a movie in the middle of the afternoon. Creativity doesn't work on a time clock.

I love the freedom to be creative—yet I have to work within deadlines. There's an energy that goes into the artwork and relaxation downtime when I'm not painting. I love it that I don't have that constant somebody looking over my shoulder when my creativity is not there.

WHAT DO YOU HATE ABOUT IT?

I don't like the business side of it such as making calls, filling out invoices… whatever, because it detracts from what I love. I don't hate it, but it's a distraction—it is a necessary evil. I don't have an agent. I read all the contracts myself, although I do have a lawyer. I do my own taxes. I do all the bookkeeping.

WHAT IS THE BIGGEST MISCONCEPTION ABOUT FREELANCING?

That it can't be done. There are generations of parents who say, "What do you want to be an artist for? Why do you want to die a poor starving artist?" What most people don't know is that the art world is very big. There are lots of companies that have studios and art departments, and those are good places to learn your craft and then move into the freelance world. You have to have a lot of confidence if you're going to be a freelancer. The work is there, but you have to find it. And you have to be good at your craft so that whatever you do will speak for itself.

LOOKING BACK ON YOUR FREELANCE CAREER, WHAT DO YOU WISH YOU HAD DONE DIFFERENTLY?

I lost a couple of copyrights on characters I created, which was a problem on my end from the business part of things. I learned about copyrights real quick after that. I guess the biggest regret is that I wish I had gotten into the freelance world earlier than I did—I might have been more successful right now.

WHAT ADVICE WOULD YOU GIVE SOMEONE WHO IS LOOKING TO START A FREELANCE CAREER?

Have confidence in yourself and your work. Make sure your work is comparable or better than the work you see available in the market you're aiming toward. Having confidence will keep your drive high and hopefully the more you do the work, the better you are going to get. You need to understand the marketplace and how you stack up. You need to be a viable commodity. If your work is substandard, you just won't get clients.

DAY IN THE LIFE OF A FREELANCE ILLUSTRATOR

6:00 a.m.   Wake up, come into the studio, and start working. Even before eating breakfast, I start working. Work four to five hours. Right now I'm working on two projects—one is a cover for a video game magazine, the other is a rush project for seven small head portraits for a gaming company—collective trading cards.

12:00 p.m.   Take a break and have lunch with my wife (she also works from home). Go out to send a piece of artwork through FedEx and run some household errands.

2:00 p.m. Back at the studio, where I keep painting for another four hours or so.

6:00 p.m. Have dinner as a family. It's the end of my work day as far as serious paint-ing or drawing is concerned. I don't like to work at night. After working for the day, I watch some TV or read a book.

10:30 p.m. Go to bed.

Actor/Writer/Film Producer/Inventor

Age: 39
Years freelancing: 14
Education: B.A. in fine and performing arts with a minor in modern dance
Hours per week: 80, including weekend work
Annual salary range: worst year, $60,000; best year, $1.4 million

WHAT DO YOU DO?

I'm an entertainer, writer, producer, and inventor. My wife and I own an entertainment production company together and I work under it to go out and perform. I do stand-up comedy and we've produced three films. I also own a company that produces a lap-top computer accessory, which I sell and promote through the website, personal appearances, and conventions.

WHAT DID YOU DO BEFORE?

Before that I was in college. I helped put myself through college as a darkroom technician and by doing stand-up comedy. I grew up in Canada.

HOW DID YOU BECOME A FREELANCER?

I always assumed I would work for myself. I had done a lot of research into the lives of comics and actors, and it seemed very romantic and freelance-y.

WHAT ARE YOUR CAREER ASPIRATIONS?

More of the same… acting, producing, writing. The cost of producing films is decreasing rapidly. It's affordable now to buy equipment to broadcast quality productions. The need for me, as a creator, is to be in cahoots with what the networks have diminished. I envision some sort of new version of my own network through the Internet as an entertainment portal. I can be shooting and producing comedy shows in my own studio—I don't need the whole monolith. So I see myself doing that.

WHAT KIND OF PEOPLE DO WELL IN FREELANCE CAREERS?

I think the one thing they have in common is the joy of curiosity. Not just being curious, but enjoying exploring and learning new things. People who are not freaked out by a big gaping nothingness in front of them. It includes all of the clichés: a self-starter, someone with discipline.

I'm always reticent when people say that freelancers don't have to answer to a boss. The quality of being "angry at the man" is not conducive to having a good freelance career. In any freelance career, you will be your own "man," and anger will turn inward.

WHAT KIND OF PEOPLE DON'T DO WELL IN FREELANCING?

A large [number] of artists need their managers to hold their hands. These are the more mocked clichés of actors—stay-at-home actors. Same for writers, too.

Those with an inability to finish things find it difficult to freelance—I know this guy who has been writing the same screenplay since I've known him.

Cubicle workers who've had it up to there and go into freelancing with a sense of arrogance may be in for a rude awakening. It's those people who stick vanity plates on their cars that have the name of their company and then sit in their sweatpants and wait for sales to come in. They won't make it. They have an illusion of what freelancing is all about. It's not reality.

WHAT DO YOU LOVE ABOUT FREELANCING?

I love the energy that flows through my office—nobody's yelling at me, and I'm not yelling at other people. I love the completely organic process of getting what's in my brain out the door for other people to start collaborating on.

And the freedom. This morning I took a friend to the airport, because I could. I get up at 6 a.m. or 10 a.m. or 4 a.m. Each day is full of different meanings, different projects— I fly out to different conventions—I enjoy the variety of it. My father worked in a union rail yard and had a habitual daily existence. In my life, no two days that are the same—this is something I treasure.

WHAT DO YOU HATE ABOUT IT?

I've been fortunate enough to buy a house with my freelance career. But dealing with the bank when you have a fluctuating annual salary is tough. You can easily attach your self-esteem to how big a loan you can get. In show business, like any other freelance career, there's always something around the corner that can make you a million dollars or wipe you out completely.

My spouse got sick of not knowing what the future held. I saw it as nomadic, and she saw it as threatening. She lived a freelance life for six or seven years. Since then she has become a registered nurse and now all of the banks will talk to us. It does help to have a spouse with a steady job.

WHAT IS THE BIGGEST MISCONCEPTION ABOUT FREELANCING?

That you get to sit around all day. There's no one here feeding me grapes.

WHAT ADVICE WOULD YOU GIVE SOMEONE WHO IS LOOKING TO START A FREELANCE CAREER?

I suggest taking evening classes at a local college that fit not only what you like to do, but will give you the skills you are lacking. There were certain things I didn't want to depend on other people to do—like bookkeeping. I learned those skills so that I could communicate with other contractors and double-check their work and know I wasn't being ripped off. My wife did as well. We do our own bookkeeping with QuickBooks and we outsource legal needs, like contracts and agents. But I do a lot myself.

A DAY IN THE LIFE OF A FREELANCE ACTOR

4:00 a.m.   Wake up. It's too early, so I stay in bed and think about my day and plan it all out.

7:00 a.m.   Drive my friend to the airport. While at airport, I pick up gas scooter that my brother-in-law couldn't get on the plane.

10:00 a.m.   Get mail at the post office.

11:00 a.m.   Get back home and walk the dog, followed by some yoga.

12:00 p.m.   Work at my desk answering emails and writing a script. Copy my comedy DVD for someone in Amsterdam who bought it. Talk with suppliers.

2:00 p.m.   Eat some fruit and vegetables and take a nap by the pool in the sun. The phone wakes me up.

2:30 p.m.   Back working. There is a production issue on a screenplay we are working on. I need to distribute the pages through email. Conduct email flight control for one hour.

3:30 p.m.   Start getting ready for an evening show. Have to wear a suit, so get that ready. Stage call is at 7 p.m.—a comedy show.

4:30 p.m.   Spend some time prepping to interview with the press. Also prep for tomorrow when I fly out for a science fiction convention. I just got a new video camera; tinker with it to make sure it works.

6:00 p.m.   Leave for my comedy show. Show's at 8 p.m. Ends at 9 p.m.

9:00 p.m.   Come back home and finish the shipping and receiving—get one of my products and DVD ready for the 6 a.m. mail. Catch some TiVo until midnight or 1 a.m., when I finally tucker out and go to bed.

Life and Business Coach

Age: 47
Years freelancing: four
Education: B.A. in psychology
Hours work per week: 30–45
Annual salary range: $50,000–$75,000

WHAT DO YOU DO?

I help people get what they want from their life through coaching. I coach people, help them build their businesses, and also write and create information products that support my coaching services.

WHAT DID YOU DO BEFORE?

I've been a women's health counselor, general manager of a retail store chain, and owned businesses (a dance studio and an office equipment store).

HOW DID YOU BECOME A FREELANCER?

I wasn't satisfied working in the women's health field. The things I love about the health field—working one-on-one with people—I couldn't do very much of at my job. My only option, it seemed, was to become a therapist and social worker, which wasn't appealing to me because I didn't want to continue to work in the current healthcare system.

I discovered life coaching quite by accident while I was on vacation and had a dream I couldn't stop thinking about. I dreamed I could fly. I asked myself, "What is stopping me from flying?" When I got home, I went on the Internet with the intention of finding a new career. Within three clicks, I found Life on Purpose Institute and said, "This is me." Within three days, I had registered into the coach-training program.

I spent a year in that training program. Toward the end of that year, I placed an ad in our local paper and started to get clients from it. After I got three clients, I left my cozy job with a paycheck and benefits, and took the plunge.

WHAT ARE YOUR CAREER ASPIRATIONS?

My vision for my business is to create more information products as passive income streams and continue to build clientele. I'd like to take on associates to help with the client load. Eventually I'd like to sell the whole thing—retirement.

WHAT KINDS OF PEOPLE DO WELL IN FREELANCE CAREERS?

People who can weather roller coasters, who have a lot of resilience and creative energy. People who are out of survival mode and have a support structure—both financially and emotionally. They need to have a strong ego and be able to hear "no" a lot and be able to fail and not have that devastate them.

WHAT KINDS OF PEOPLE DON'T DO WELL IN FREELANCING?

People who can't handle risk or who need a lot of externally imposed structure.

WHAT DO YOU LOVE ABOUT FREELANCING?

That I did it. That whatever I experience is a direct result of my efforts, that the buck stops with me. I want to say that I like the freedom, but I'm not sure if there's much freedom. But that's my choice. I like the flexibility; I can take time off when I want to and work weekends if I need to. I also like being a positive model of what is possible to others. I like that people can look at me and say, "Wow, she did it—maybe I can do it, too."

WHAT DO YOU HATE ABOUT IT?

I hate the volatility. Everything is based on what you do or don't do. This may be particular to my industry, but in my business, I have to deal with the fact that human nature takes the path of least resistance and people cancel appointments. If I get enough cancellations, that can mean the difference between a great month and a survival month. Another challenge is always having to keep my pipeline filled. I can never relax fully.

WHAT IS THE BIGGEST MISCONCEPTION ABOUT FREELANCING?

That you can make a ton of money and it's easy.

LOOKING BACK ON YOUR FREELANCE CAREER, WHAT DO YOU WISH YOU HAD DONE DIFFERENTLY?

I wish I made a more gradual transition to no paycheck. I could have done it part-time much longer. I wish I had moved out of my comfort zone faster and became more of a public person sooner [by networking].

WHAT ADVICE WOULD YOU GIVE SOMEONE WHO IS LOOKING TO START A FREELANCE CAREER?

Don't quit your day job so fast. You need to make sure you have a way to support yourself for the first year. You also need to have an emotional or professional support system of people to connect with. You really have to have a methodology to what you are going to do, not just doing the technician part of your job. Be prepared for it to take three to four years until you can determine if the business is working or not.

A DAY IN THE LIFE OF A BUSINESS AND LIFE COACH

6:30 a.m.   Wake up and go to the gym. Come home for a bagel with my husband.

9:00 a.m.   Answer personal emails—I'm trying to sell a car online—and pay bills.

10:00 a.m.   Client appointment.

11:00 a.m.   Media interview.

12:00 p.m.   Two back-to-back client appointments.

1:45 p.m.   Meet a friend for lunch.

3:00 p.m.   Another client appointment.

4:00 p.m.   Work on editing some writing projects.

5:00 p.m.   Last client appointment of the day.

6:00 p.m.   Wrap up the day and answer last-minute emails.

6:30 p.m.   Time to eat dinner and hang out with my family.

Business Consultant

Years freelancing: two
Education: B.S. in geology, MBA
Hours per week: 40
Annual salary range: $25,000–50,000

WHAT DO YOU DO?

I work with organizations to help them make better use of their resources. The problem is that many organizations don't know how to approach projects and they actually don't know how to make good use of their people. Most business meetings are a terrible waste of time where nothing gets done, no decisions are made, and nobody knows what they are supposed to do as a result of the meeting.

I conduct two-hour workshops for companies in which I give every individual in the class the tools they need to facilitate good productive meetings. My clients include three-person companies all the way up to 1,000-employee companies.

WHAT DID YOU DO BEFORE?

I spent 12 years (total) at a Fortune 500 tech company working in sales and technical support and then in data center operations. I spent six years doing very technical work—system administration and system programming. Because I had both technical and people skills, I was asked to start leading projects. I took a lot of training classes through the company and became a project management professional. Then I became a certified project manager.

HOW DID YOU BECOME A FREELANCER?

I was laid off. I was single—in better shape compared to my teammates who had families and mortgages. And, I was ready for a change. This allowed me to have a good chunk of time to figure out where I wanted to live and what I wanted to do. I moved closer to my family. After much thought, I realized I wanted to go to work for myself.

I think the first obstacle in any freelance endeavor is feeling confident enough to go into a business and say (to a potential client), "Yes, I can help you." Joining a business-networking group was helpful for me in that initial startup phase getting in front of people. What really built my confidence was actually doing the work and seeing that I was able to improve people's work life and reduce stress, and seeing people's gratitude for the work I had done. This bolstered my confidence.

WHAT ARE YOUR CAREER ASPIRATIONS?

Right now I spend a lot of time marketing my business, which seems appropriate for the second year of business. But I would like to be recognized in this region as a trusted adviser. I would like to spend less of my time marketing and more of my time doing the work.

WHAT KINDS OF PEOPLE DO WELL IN FREELANCE CAREERS?

People who have a sense of confidence. So many people talk themselves into feeling bad. The only difference between me and someone who's in a job they hate and feel like they can't leave is that I'm willing to put myself in front of people. I'm not easily embarrassed or afraid to make a fool of myself. But I do have to give myself pep talks before big events.

People who go into freelance work can't be risk-averse. I'm risk-seeking; I ride a motorcycle; I've moved to brand-new towns many times in my life; I thrive on change and trying out new things. So that means in my work, I'm willing to take on projects that may be different from anything I've ever done before.

People also need to be a quick study and learn things fast, and size up situations pretty quickly.

WHAT KINDS OF PEOPLE DON'T DO WELL IN FREELANCING?

People who procrastinate. People who get scared easily, either by uneven cash flow and insecurity or fear of new situations. People who are scared of being creative. I think that part of working freelance, or consulting, is that you have to be willing to be creative on the fly. Working with human beings means you never quite know what's going to happen.

WHAT DO YOU REALLY LOVE ABOUT YOUR BUSINESS?

I love feeling like I'm the best person to help these folks out. I spent long enough in corporate America to understand my clients and know how bad it can be in terms of stress and uncertainty and being given responsibility without authority. I have a lot of empathy and really enjoy being able to help.

I love feeling that I control my work life. I control my schedule and whom I work with. I also like the fact that I come into a company from the outside and can point things out that people on the inside can't do for political reasons. I feel it is my duty to point out these problems. This is the piece I love the most about not being part of corporate America: I don't have to pretend that certain problems don't exist.

WHAT DO YOU HATE ABOUT BEING A FREELANCER?

I hate the feeling that I have to do everything myself. I'm my own financial consultant, bookkeeper, and secretary. I have recently hired a virtual assistant, which has totally changed my work life. Even though I use her only nine to ten hours a month, it has doubled my output. She has helped with posters, direct mail, putting together a registration spreadsheet, making a PowerPoint template. She says the things she loves to do are all the things I hate to do.

Another piece I dislike is the uneven cash flow. I can get four to five months' worth of income in one month. Then there are some months when no money is coming in. However, like I said, I'm only in my second year, and the potential for my business seems excellent. I can see myself with more work than I can do.

WHAT IS THE BIGGEST MISCONCEPTION ABOUT FREELANCING?

That it's easy, or that the work will find you. There's so much you have to do to put yourself out there. Another misconception is that you can hit the ground running from day one.

LOOKING BACK ON YOUR FREELANCE CAREER, WHAT DO YOU WISH YOU HAD DONE DIFFERENTLY?

I wish I had done a brochure earlier. It has been really helpful to have a nice-looking brochure to hand out.

I wish I had written a business plan. I still haven't done it. The value isn't in having the written document; it's the thinking that goes behind it. It is still on my to-do list.

DO YOU HAVE ADVICE FOR PEOPLE CONTEMPLATING A FREELANCING CAREER?

Get good at something. That is a requirement because you can't have a freelance career in something you're not good at. Make sure you get the education, certification, and experience. And write a business plan.

Make sure you network. When you're starting from scratch, you need all the help you can get, so don't isolate yourself.

A DAY IN THE LIFE OF A FREELANCE BUSINESS CONSULTANT

5:30 a.m.	Wake up, check email, eat breakfast.
7:30 a.m.	Attend a Business Network International meeting.
9:30 a.m.	Meet with potential clients.
11:00 a.m.	Back at the office to check email.
12:00 p.m.	Have lunch with my virtual assistant to talk about plans for next month.
1:30 p.m.	Take a bike ride.
4:00 p.m.	Work on upcoming presentation.
7:00 p.m.	Relax for a bit to have dinner and listen to some music.
9:00 p.m.	Continue work on upcoming presentation.
11:00 p.m.	Bedtime.

Virtual Assistant

Age: 39
Years freelancing: one
Education: B.S. in information systems
Hours work per week: 35–40
Annual salary range: Under $25,000

WHAT DO YOU DO?

I provide administrative and business support to small business owners. Administration encompasses a huge bucket of tasks such as accounting, weekly cash flow reports, mail merges, PowerPoint presentations, ordering supplies, getting workbooks ready, handouts, doctors' appointments, or monitoring phone and email messages. I do a lot of work with Excel worksheets, various reports, and simple graphic design work.

WHAT DID YOU DO BEFORE?

I've been in the workforce for 20 years and have done a lot of different things. I've worked in retail, wholesale, printing, direct mail marketing, and software development, and I've been an executive assistant. I have always been in support roles, and I like that. I've never been driven for the manager slot. What I like is keeping things in the right place. I enjoy that, so this work is a natural fit for me.

HOW DID YOU BECOME A FREELANCER?

My husband died of cancer. That was a very hard year for me. I had to regroup. I went back to work for a year in a bank until I received life insurance benefits. I needed stability and structure during that time, and it was good to work. When I got the life insurance, I bailed on the bank. I had gotten an email about a virtual assistant program before my husband died, and it was always in the back of my mind. So, I decided to sign up and work part-time. It took five months to get the training, and right after I completed it, I started doing marketing. Three months later, I had my first client. By then I had remarried.

WHAT ARE YOUR CAREER ASPIRATIONS?

I would like, ideally, to have six retainer clients. Right now I have a choice of pay-as-you-go or going on retainer for ten hours a month. With the pay-as-you-go, business can be chaotic, with a ton of work one month and then nothing next month. Ideally, I'd like a full practice of retainer clients.

WHAT KINDS OF PEOPLE DO WELL IN FREELANCE CAREERS?

I'm not the kind of person you'd think would go freelance. I'm a very structured, routine-oriented person. I like security; I like to plan things. Being a freelancer doesn't lend itself to those qualities, so I get unnerved at times. However, when you've lost someone you love, it puts a whole new spin on things. I think that's what gave me courage, because what's the worst thing that can happen in a business? You fail. After the death of my husband, failing at a business didn't seem so catastrophic.

People who do well in freelancing seem to like a little chaos in their lives; they like the thrill. I don't particularly like that and I work hard to overcome it—I struggle with that almost on a daily basis. It would probably be much easier to go someplace to work every day, but I have so much fun meeting people through my business. I keep reminding myself how much fun I'm having.

WHAT KINDS OF PEOPLE DON'T DO WELL IN FREELANCING?

People who need a lot of control, because you can't control who is going to call you or when a client will sign. You need to be able to go with the flow. If you are too controlling, you can frustrate yourself pretty quickly.

WHAT DO YOU LOVE ABOUT FREELANCING?

Freelancing is a double-edged sword. I love being able to go into yoga and then go into work late. But I still have the responsibility of keeping my client base.

WHAT DO YOU HATE ABOUT FREELANCING?

The worst thing is clients who are slow-paying. I hate chasing the money. I'm not in this to be a collection agency. The check is due immediately, and they need to mail it to me. But because of the nature of my relationship with my clients (we tend to be close), it is a very awkward thing to ask for my money.

I hate that I worry about where the client base is coming from. Right now, though, I'm so busy I don't know what to do with myself. That's why I'm trying to shape the business to the ideal retainer practice I'm looking for.

WHAT IS THE BIGGEST MISCONCEPTION ABOUT FREELANCING?

That it's all a cakewalk and all fun and games. There are just as many downsides as upsides. To do this, you need to appreciate the upsides enough to offset the downsides.

WHAT ADVICE WOULD YOU GIVE SOMEONE WHO IS LOOKING TO START A FREELANCE CAREER?

Do a business plan. It's awful to do, but it really helps. Study your target market. Check out the rules and regulations in your state and town. Do your homework.

A DAY IN THE LIFE OF A FREELANCE VIRTUAL ASSISTANT

7:30 a.m.   Wake up, get dressed, and have breakfast.

8:00 a.m.   Conduct a client training on QuickBooks.

9:00 a.m.   Check emails to see if anything urgent needs a response; make cup of tea.

9:30 a.m.   Polish a PowerPoint presentation for a client. Get up every hour to stretch, let the cat out, let the cat back in, walk out to the mailbox, and so on.

12:30 p.m.   Prepare PDF files of handouts for a client to send out to a printer. Send everything to the client via email.

2:00 p.m.   Call my Web hosting company with questions to work out for client stuff. Do some research for a client on email issues for a mutual Web hosting company. Check email.

3:00 p.m.   Time gets eaten up with email exchanges. Through email, set up a time to meet with a client, importing data into the client's Outlook. Review more email. Fiddle with the new phone system. Import all my jobs from my Day-Timer into QuickBooks to get a pulse on where I am with retainer clients.

4:00 p.m.   Close of business. Typically, I allot 9 a.m. to 4 p.m. to my office work. My husband comes home; have a glass of wine with him.

6:00 p.m.   Have dinner with my husband.

6:15 p.m.   A client calls to email a file. I don't pick up the phone, but listen to the message; send the file after dinner. I try to serve my clients well without sacrificing my boundaries. I make it very clear I'm not available 24/7.

8:00 p.m.   Go to bed and read.

Animal Communicator

Age: 49

Years freelancing: three

Education: B.S. in nursing; certificate in holistic nursing; certificate in Reiki I; fellowship in holistic nursing; various other workshops and training

Hours per week: 25–40, or more

Annual salary range: Under $25,000, but growing steadily (charges $25 per 15-minute increment)

WHAT DO YOU DO?

I'm an animal communicator, better known as a pet psychic. My profession has gotten a lot more credibility because of Animal Planet's pet psychic. I see myself as a bridge between people and animals. I talk to a client's animal and give the client information they can work with. I usually do this with my eyes closed and can do this over the telephone. How does it work? I will get bodily sensations, so if an animal's stomach is upset, my stomach will get upset. Usually I get a whole download of stuff, everything from bodily sensations to emotions. I have to tell you that most dogs don't think I'm such a big deal, and this really hurt my ego in the beginning.

WHAT DID YOU DO BEFORE?

I was a nurse for 25 years. I started out in surgical intensive care units, and my last position was in cardiac rehab.

HOW DID YOU BECOME A FREELANCER?

It was an accident: I got laid off. And I was so angry that I did a lot of ranting. One day my husband said, "Oh, be quiet and decide what you want to do when you grow up." This was good advice and I decided I was going to be a family dog trainer. That's why I got trained in Bailey & Bailey Operant Conditioning. But family dog training never fell into place; while it looked great on paper, the business never went everywhere. At this point, I was already communicating with my own dogs, but not in the same way as animal communicators. I just needed training—and permission to do this without it being weird. So I got trained by a specialist in the mechanics of it.

WHAT ARE YOUR CAREER ASPIRATIONS?

This is my future. I think my practice will evolve into some kind of healing practice along with animal communication, using more and more of my nursing skills. My business, when it expands, won't be in my home space. It feels very invasive to have people come to my home with their animals.

WHAT KINDS OF PEOPLE DO WELL IN FREELANCE CAREERS?

You need to be able to set a plan and carry it through while still being free enough to adjust it as necessary. When you're working for someone else, you are carrying out their plan, which takes a lot off your shoulders so you don't have to figure it all out. [When you're] working for yourself, you have to figure it all out, such as what you're good at, what you're willing to learn to be good or adequate at, what you're not good at, and what you're willing to pay someone to do.

I do have a [freelance] marketing person… who did my brochure, business cards, and advertising poster template, and who designed a vinyl banner for me to use at dog shows.

To be successful, no matter what kind of freelancer you are, you really have to like people. I had a wonderful Doberman who I learned a lot from: He thought that people were the most marvelous joke on the face of the earth. Now, when clients get weird, I don't get uptight. I just think, "Ha, what a joke." You have to be pleasant even when you don't feel like it, because your attitude really translates to your bottom line.

You also have to love what you're doing because sometimes it's a giant pain in the ass. But if it's something you really believe in, all the hours you have to put in don't matter.

You have to know when to say no and stick to it. You have to draw the line somewhere and keep it. If you're a people-pleaser, you're doomed, because you'll be sucked dry.

WHAT KINDS OF PEOPLE DON'T DO WELL IN FREELANCING?

People who are easily discouraged. People who can't see any alternative besides plan A. And people who take it all personally.

You need to be flexible. Sometimes you don't have much business, and you have a lot of free time. So you can go for a long walk or take your elderly mother to her appointment. On the other hand, sometimes you are busy with stuff you don't want to do, like accounting. You need to know when to farm it out to someone else. You have to be able to adjust to being busy and then not being so busy, and enjoy one while enduring the other.

WHAT DO YOU LOVE ABOUT FREELANCING?

I like the flexibility. I don't mind slack periods, except they make me a little nervous. I like the fact that even when I mess up, it's all mine. I do my best, and if it works fine, I learn from it. There's nobody telling me I'm wrong before I even start. I like that I can work in my PJs now, and I don't have to be out the door at a certain time looking radiant, which some days was quite a challenge.

WHAT DO YOU HATE ABOUT IT?

I hate being green at anything. Sometimes I hate it only being me. As you can imagine, there aren't that many people around in my profession to bounce ideas off of and who really understand what I'm talking about. Initially, I hated looking for all of the services I needed, like someone to write copy or a printer. But it has all been a learning experience, and no learning is ever wasted.

In the beginning, I had a really difficult time feeling confident about the service I was providing and the rate I was charging. I'm getting much better at it, but it was very hard at first. It's easy to state a set price on behalf of an employer, but very hard on behalf of yourself.

WHAT IS THE BIGGEST MISCONCEPTION ABOUT FREELANCING?

That you make tons of money. You don't realize how many taxes an employer pays on your behalf. Now I have to pay Social Security and Medicare; I have to pay it all, and it's ugly. The second greatest misconception is that because you're the boss, you can do whatever you want. You have to do things that are right for the business and right for you. It's freedom with a catch.

Another misconception is that freelancing is easy. People don't realize there's a lot of hidden work not apparent until you have to produce it. You have to decide how you are going to answer the telephone and you have to do it the same [way] all the time. You need to decide about paperwork and how you will bill people, and how you'll keep your schedule.

LOOKING BACK ON YOUR FREELANCE CAREER, WHAT DO YOU WISH YOU HAD DONE DIFFERENTLY?

I wish I had gone to QuickBooks right away, because it's such a nice program.

WHAT ADVICE WOULD YOU GIVE SOMEONE WHO IS LOOKING TO START A FREELANCE CAREER?

Remember that it takes longer than you think. It takes a good solid five years to become an overnight sensation. In my business, the trust and safety factor is huge. Clients don't know at first if I'm weird or safe. There's always that question: "Is she a wild-eyed nut or a normal person with this talent and ability?" People need to see me face-to-face. Word of mouth has been my most valuable advertisement.

A DAY IN THE LIFE OF A FREELANCE ANIMAL COMMUNICATOR

6:00 a.m.   Wake up. Let out the dogs; my husband and I have three dogs and one visiting. Put the water on for tea.

7:00 a.m.   Check email. If anybody wants an appointment, I do that first. Handle updates on a client. Meditate for 20 minutes. Do laundry. Morning is the time when I do mindless tasks while my mind is in neutral; I like to see what bubbles up.

8:00 a.m.   Enter receipts from the day before. Go to the bank and to the post office. Walk the dogs.

10:00 a.m.   Do more paperwork, and then eat lunch. After lunch, I do some agility training with my dogs.

2:00 p.m.   Telephone appointment with an older client who has horse troubles; this woman is afraid of her horse and doesn't know why. Her horse is very sweet and cooporative, but both horse and rider are inexperienced. After that, I have another telephone interview with a client who has a dog that is acting oddly. The dog is blind. To me, it feels like there is something in the nervous system going on, like a stroke or pressure on part of the brain. Times like this is when my nursing background comes in handy. But I'm not a vet. Sometimes, when things feel really bad, I suggest that clients visit their vet. Sometimes I can tell if a chiropractor will fix it. I do suggest a vet for this client's dog.

4:30 p.m.   Dogs get fed. Then make supper and do household tasks.

6:00 p.m.   My evening appointments begin at this time. I have one client with a small poodle mix that came from a shelter. This dog has a condition where she doesn't make enough blood platelets. I want to know from the dog what is going on. The client wants to ask the dog, "Are you going to die and leave me soon?" To which the dog says, "No, I'm not going anywhere, and you better not leave me." This is a cool dog. If she were human, she'd be a biker chick. Then I have another telephone appointment with a client who has a Bichon dog; she wants a 15-minute check-in about the dog's allergies.

8:00 p.m.   Finish up work and go to bed. This work takes up a lot of energy and I need a lot of sleep.

Graphic Designer

Age: 46
Years freelancing: ten
Education: B.A in fine arts
Hours per week: 15–30
Annual salary range: $50,000–75,000

WHAT DO YOU DO?

I'm a graphic designer. I design print materials and websites for businesses that need to communicate a message for advertising or marketing. I also design newsletters.

WHAT DID YOU DO BEFORE?

I was a jewelry designer. After college I worked as a typesetter for a company that published computer magazines, but I never embraced the corporate life. I was a little bored and restless there. But while there, I saw some earrings in a store that I liked and couldn't afford and I thought I'd make some. I started making jewelry and brought it to work and people purchased it. After doing both jobs full-time, I switched to doing jewelry full-time. It was fun but a hard way to make a living.

HOW DID YOU BECOME A FREELANCER?

After I had a child, I started to get really tired. I didn't have a community in my own town because I was away so much at trade shows. So I started to brainstorm ideas on what I could do at home. I gave myself a year to decide and even kept a notebook. Ideas ranged from making homemade spaghetti sauce to being a land surveyor. But all along my strongest idea was to be a graphic designer. I took a class one semester, but had a nursing baby and I couldn't wait in lines to use the lab computers. I had to decide if I would continue, because I had to invest in $5,000 worth of computer equipment. So I invested in the equipment, completed my studies, and started my business.

WHAT ARE YOUR CAREER ASPIRATIONS?

Lately, my business has taken an unexpected turn and I am functioning more like an agency without having made a decision to grow my business. I have subcontracted a database coordinator and designer and am putting together a website for a hospital. This might end up being a niche that is good for me. If I continue in this direction, my business will be more profitable. I'd like to have a good business to sell when I'm older. My decision to start this business was mostly about money, because my passions lie elsewhere.

WHAT KINDS OF PEOPLE DO WELL IN FREELANCE CAREERS?

People who are flexible, and who are willing to take the ups and downs of being a freelancer. People who don't get too stressed out by the low periods or the really busy periods. It's important to keep it in perspective.

People who can keep themselves on task. If you are working at home, it is so easy to get distracted by household tasks, electricians coming in, or kids who are sick.

You also need to be creative—and brave. You need to get out there in the world and toot your own horn. You need to be self-confident to give others confidence in your abilities; you need to exude the aura of "I know what I'm doing, and it's worth hiring me for a lot of money to do it."

WHAT KINDS OF PEOPLE DON'T DO WELL IN FREELANCING?

If you're low on confidence or if you're terribly shy, or extremely disorganized, you might have a hard time being a successful freelancer. People who are not personable won't do well. And neither will people who crave security, or regularity. If you have a strong need for predictable regular work flow and income, freelancing may not be for you.

WHAT DO YOU LOVE ABOUT FREELANCING?

I like that I'm the boss. And I like that it's unpredictable because I think I'd get bored doing the same thing over and over. It doesn't matter if you're in a creative business or not—owning a business is a creative thing and I like the creativity involved in running it. I like being in my own office in my own home. A lot of my clients come to me because they are friends or friends of friends, so I get to work with great people whom I admire. Working with people is number one. What's really fun is coming up with a good product that satisfies the need of a client. Graphic design is fun in isolation, but it's much more fun with the client. Lastly, I love that it enables me to be flexible for my kids.

WHAT DO YOU HATE ABOUT FREELANCING?

I hate it when business is slow and I'm trying to scrounge up new work. However, that doesn't happen as often since I'm more established. On the flip side, when it's really busy, it's hard to stay organized and maintain your systems, and it gets hard for me to concentrate. I end up wondering if it is all really under control. That's when I try to slow down and get everything in order. But overall, it's pleasant working for myself.

WHAT IS THE BIGGEST MISCONCEPTION ABOUT FREELANCING?

People think that you have more leisure and leeway than you actually do. On one hand, your clients can be breathing down your neck, but you can still go out to lunch. But still, you're not as free as you appear. People think it's cushy, but it's not. Not if you want to be successful.

LOOKING BACK ON YOUR FREELANCE CAREER, WHAT DO YOU WISH YOU HAD DONE DIFFERENTLY?

Part of me wishes I had become a teacher, working with kids, in a job that has some security and health insurance. For my family, health insurance is a huge cost and problem right now; we haven't been able to save money for our future.

WHAT ADVICE WOULD YOU GIVE SOMEONE WHO IS LOOKING TO START A FREELANCE CAREER?

Talk to lots of people and ask lots of questions. Invest in equipment you need. And make sure you write a business plan.

A DAY IN THE LIFE OF A FREELANCE GRAPHIC DESIGNER

6:30 a.m.   Wake up and go downstairs to make my son's lunch for school. Empty the dishwasher. Take a shower and get the kids up for school and cart them there.

8:30 a.m.   Come home and finish eating breakfast and cleaning up.

9:00 a.m.   Go upstairs to my office and answer email and make some phone calls. Prioritize my list for the day.

9:30 a.m.   Look at the developing website for my hospital client. I have a few questions so I email the subcontractor. I send a note to the client that the unresolved issues would be resolved in a few days.

10:15 a.m.   Go to an exercise class.

11:30 a.m.   Get home and make lunch. Eat alone in my office.

12:30 p.m.   Work on a label for a skincare product package. I'm trying out a few different ideas. Send out the rough draft to the client for input.

1:45 p.m.   Phone rings. It's a friend with a personal problem. While on phone, pick up another call from my daughter's piano teacher. Try to continue working while on the phone with both people on both lines, but make mistakes on the work that I have to go back and fix.

2:00 p.m.   Call a prospective client interested in a website design. Get specifications and tell him I will call back to set up a meeting.

2:15 p.m.   Make myself a cup of tea.

2:30 p.m.   Work on a newsletter design. Get some photos off the Web, crop them with Photoshop, and place them in the newsletter format.

3:15 p.m.   Pick up the kids from school, along with some of the kids' friends for a play date. The babysitter arrives for afternoon childcare.

3:30 p.m.   Client arrives for a meeting; we meet in the office. We finish up final edits on an annual report. After the client leaves, I prepare computer files for the printer and copy them onto a CD for the client to take to the printer.

5:00 p.m.   Go downstairs, send babysitter home, and start cooking dinner.

6:00 p.m.   Husband comes home, and we all eat dinner together.

7:00 p.m.   Play catch with the kids in the yard.

7:30 p.m.   Bedtime routine for the kids. Finish cleaning dishes. Check email one last time.

9:45 p.m.   Go to bed and watch *West Wing*.

11:00 p.m.   Snooze time.

For Your Reference

Self-Assessment Tools

Self-Employment Associations

Federal and State Government Resources

Online Networking Sites

Freelancing Job Boards

Other Job Boards

Recommended Reading

Self-Assessment Tools

The MAPP Test

http://www.assessment.com/MAPPMembers/Welcome.asp?accnum=06-5413-000.00

The Motivational Appraisal of Personal Potential (MAPP) test focuses on your personal career motivation priorities and your preferred styles of communication, learning, and leadership.

The Princeton Review Career Quiz

http://www.princetonreview.com/cte/quiz/career_quiz1.asp

The Princeton Review Career Quiz is a fast, 24-question quiz that presents you with some interesting career suggestions based on your social and working style.

People, Data, Things Quiz

http://www.jobsetc.ca/toolbox/quizzes/dpt_quiz.do?lang=e

Put out by the Government of Canada, this test assesses how you see yourself working with the three main components of any job: people, data, and things.

The Career Interests Game

http://career.missouri.edu/modules.php?name=News&file=article&sid=146

The Career Interests Game is an exercise based on Dr. John L. Holland's theory that people and work environments can be loosely classified into six different groups. It's designed to help match your interests/skills with careers.

The Career Key

http://www.careerkey.org/cgi-bin/ck.pl?action=choices

The Career Key is designed to tell you your "Holland Code" and the possible occupations that match your strengths.

Dr. John L. Holland's Self-Directed Search

http://www.self-directed-search.com

Dr. John L. Holland's Self-Directed Search (SDS) test asks very specific questions regarding your interests, skills, and perceived career fits. You can take his test free on the Web—an analysis of the results, however, will cost you $9.95.

Highlands Ability Battery

http://www.highlandsprogram.com

This in-depth assessment program provides detailed personality analysis based on hands-on work samples. The assessment measures seven personality factors that combine to make the whole person. The cost is generally in the $300 to $400 range.

Self-Employment Associations

- Professional Association of Contract Employees (http://www.pacepros.com)

- American Association of Home-Based Business (http://www.aahbb.org)

- Home Office Association of America (http://www.hoaa.com)

- National Association for the Self-Employed (http://www.nase.org)

Federal and State Government Resources

- IRS Employer Identification Number (EIN) Questionnaire (http://www.irs.gov/businesses/small/article/0,,id=98350,00.html)

- Local IRS Field Office Contacts (http://www.irs.gov/localcontacts)

- IRS Business and Specialty Tax Hotline (800-829-4933)

- IRS Publication 505: Tax Withholding and Estimated Tax (http://www.irs.gov/pub/irs-pdf/p505.pdf)

- IRS Helpline (800-829-1040, ext. 9825)

- U.S. Patent and Trademark Office's trademark page (http://www.uspto.gov/main/trademarks.htm)

Online Networking Sites

- Ecademy (http://www.ecademy.com)

- LinkedIn (http://www.linkedin.com)

- Meetup (http://www.meetup.com)

- Ryze (http://www.ryze.com)

- Tribe.net (http://www.tribe.net)

- Womans-Net (http://womans-net.com)

Freelancing Job Boards

Some of these sites ask that you fill out a registration form with your contact information before you search opportunities. Make sure you read the terms of use and privacy policies.

- Elance (http://www.elance.com)

- Freelance.com—information technology only (http://www.freelance.com)

- Guru.com (http://www.guru.com)

- HireAbility (http://www.hireability.com)

- Job-Hunt.org (http://www.job-hunt.org/free.shtml)

- Net-Temps (http://www.net-temps.com)

- Freelance Moms (http://freelancemom.com/gigs.htm)

Other Job Boards

Make sure you put in "freelance" or "contract work" when you are searching.

- CareerBuilder.com (http://www.careerbuilder.com)

- CareerJournal (http://www.careerjournal.com)

- CareerMag (http://www.careermag.com)

- Craigslist (http://www.craigslist.org)

- Job Bank USA (http://jobbankusa.com)

- Monster.com (http://www.monster.com)

- NationJob (http://www.nationjob.com)

- Yahoo! HotJobs (http://hotjobs.yahoo.com)

Freelancing Information Resources

- Working Solo (http://www.workingsolo.com)

- All Freelance Work (http://www.allfreelancework.com)

- Solo Entrepreneur Community (http://www.solo-e.com/community)

- Work-at-Home Moms (http://www.wahm.com)

Recommended Reading

GETTING STARTED

Successful Freelancing
Marian Faux (St. Martin's Press, 1997)
Tips on managing your money, your clients, and yourself.

Free Agent Nation
Daniel Pink (Warner Business Books, 2002)
An inspirational book that explains the trend toward independent contract work.

The Best Home-Based Businesses for the 21st Century
Paul and Sarah Edwards (Tarcher, 1999)
A comprehensive look at more than 100 hot new businesses that promise the top opportunities for small-business people in the future.

Complete Idiot's Guide to Starting a Home-Based Business
Barbara Weltman (Alpha, 2000)
How to set up, run, and grow a home-based business.

TAXES & LAWS

IRS Rules for Independent Contractors
(http://www.irs.ustreas.gov/businesses/small/article/0,,id=115041,00.html)

Working for Yourself: Laws & Taxes for Independent Contactors, Freelancers & Consultants
Stephen Fishman, Esq. (Nolo Press, 2003)
An independent contractor himself, the author guides you through everything you need to know about laws and taxes for your small business.

J.K. Lasser's Taxes Made Easy for Your Home-Based Business

Gary Carter (Wiley, 2002)

This book clarifies the current tax environment with regard to home-based businesses and shows you how to make the most of the new tax laws.

FOR PARENTS

Mompreneurs

Patricia Cobe and Ellen Parlapiano (Pedigree Books, 2002)

How to start a home business and take care of your children. The guide includes inspiring tales of mothers whose businesses are now household names.

How to Raise a Family and Career Under One Roof

Lisa Roberts (Brookhaven, 1997)

Real-life experience and practical advice on how to juggle your family and freelance life.

MARKETING ADVICE

The Free Agent Marketing Guide: 100+ Marketing Tips for Free Agents, Independent Consultants, and Freelancers

Douglas Florzak, (Logical Directions, Inc., 2004)

Getting Business to Come to You

Paul and Sarah Edwards (Tarcher, 1998)

How small businesses can attract customers.

HOME OFFICE HELP

101 Home Office Success Secrets

Lisa Kanarek (Career Press, 2000)

Tips include how to streamline your office, develop strong personal work habits, and get inexpensive, yet effective PR.

Organizing Your Home Business
Lisa Kanarek (Made E-Z Products, 2002)
A complete and up-to-date guide for those who are setting up home offices.

Working Solo
Terri Lonier (Wiley, 1998)
Help on how to weigh the pros and cons of going solo.

Author Bio

Marcia Passos Duffy has been a freelancer for more than ten years. She is an award-winning writer, a personal historian, and publisher of her own online magazine, *The Heart of New England* (http://www.theheartofnewengland.com). She lives and works happily under one roof with her husband, two children, a dog, and three cats in Keene, New Hampshire.

WETFEET'S INSIDER GUIDE SERIES

Job Search Guides

Getting Your Ideal Internship

International MBA Student's Guide to the U.S. Job Search

Job Hunting A to Z: Landing the Job You Want

Killer Consulting Resumes!

Killer Cover Letters & Resumes!

Killer Investment Banking Resumes!

Negotiating Your Salary & Perks

Networking Works!

Interview Guides

Ace Your Case: Consulting Interviews

Ace Your Case II: 15 More Consulting Cases

Ace Your Case III: Practice Makes Perfect

Ace Your Case IV: The Latest & Greatest

Ace Your Case V: Return to the Case Interview

Ace Your Case VI: Mastering the Case Interview

Ace Your Interview!

Beat the Street: Investment Banking Interviews

Beat the Street II: I-Banking Interview Practice Guide

Career & Industry Guides

Careers in Accounting

Careers in Advertising & Public Relations

Careers in Asset Management & Retail Brokerage

Careers in Biotech & Pharmaceuticals

Careers in Brand Management

Careers in Consumer Products

Careers in Entertainment & Sports

Careers in Health Care

Careers in Human Resources

Careers in Information Technology

Careers in Investment Banking

Careers in Management Consulting

Careers in Marketing & Market Research

Careers in Nonprofits & Government Agencies

Careers in Real Estate

Careers in Retail

Careers in Sales

Careers in Supply Chain Management

Careers in Venture Capital

Industries & Careers for MBAs

Industries & Careers for Undergrads

Million Dollar Careers

Specialized Consulting Careers: Health Care, Human Resources, and Information Technology

Company Guides

25 Top Consulting Firms

25 Top Financial Services Firms

Accenture

Bain & Company

Booz Allen Hamilton

Boston Consulting Group

Credit Suisse First Boston

Deloitte Consulting

Deutsche Bank

The Goldman Sachs Group

J.P. Morgan Chase & Co.

McKinsey & Company

Merrill Lynch & Co.

Morgan Stanley

UBS AG

WetFeet in the City Guides

Job Hunting in New York City

Job Hunting in San Francisco